Know That You Are Loved

Self-Healing Techniques for Everyone

D0584377

First published by O Books, 2010
O Books is an imprint of John Hunt Publishing Ltd., The Bothy, Deershot Lodge, Park Lane, Ropley,
Hants, SO24 0BE, UK
office1@o-books.net
www.o-books.net

Distribution in:

UK and Europe
Orca Book Services
orders@orcabookservices.co.uk
Tel: 01202 665432 Fax: 01202 666219
Int. code (44)

USA and Canada
NBN
custserv@nbnbooks.com
Tel: 1 800 462 6420 Fax: 1 800 338 4550

Australia and New Zealand
Brumby Books
sales@brumbybooks.com.au
Tel: 61 3 9761 5535 Fax: 61 3 9761 7095

Far East (offices in Singapore, Thailand,
Hong Kong, Taiwan)
Pansing Distribution Pte Ltd
kemal@pansing.com
Tel: 65 6319 9939 Fax: 65 6462 5761

South Africa
Stephan Phillips (pty) Ltd
Email: orders@stephanphillips.com
Tel: 27 21 4489839 Telefax: 27 21 4479879

Text copyright Philena Bruce 2009

Design: Stuart Davies

ISBN: 978 1 84694 308 9

A CIP catalogue record for this book is available
from the British Library.

Printed by Digital Book Print

O Books operates a distinctive and ethical publishing philosophy in
all areas of its business, from its global network of authors to
production and worldwide distribution.

Know That You Are Loved

Self-Healing Techniques for Everyone

Philena Bruce

BOOKS

Winchester, UK
Washington, USA

CONTENTS

Exercises

"This book is an absolute joy to read. I know the exercises Philena has devised work because I had a relationship healing with her over twenty years ago, which changed my life dramatically. Know That You Are Loved holds the key to connecting with the underlying fabric of the ever changing world we live in: unconditional love."
Sahar Huneidi, Author, Spiritual Life Coach columnist, Editor of PS-Magazine.com, and podcaster

"Know That You Are Loved is a delightful little book to keep handy. I enjoyed reading all the varied accounts of meaningful life lessons presented in a light hearted and candid manner. This is a practical book loaded with very useful information and advice on many aspects of life. Philena Bruce is a seasoned Healer and a good story teller with a disarming sense of humor."
Chidi Asika-Enahoro, Author, Talk Show Host & a Sr. Disability Analyst, www.loveandbalance.com

"Philena Bruce shows us common sense ways to steer through life's tangles and teaches us how to stand tall with the blessings of the sacred universe around our shoulders."
Caitlin Matthews, Author of The Psychic Protection Handbook & Singing the Soul Back Home.

"Philena's passionate love for her work has brought a wonderful series of results to many people in as many places in the world. Above all, she has a masterly touch as a raconteuse. Her "worms" in Calcutta are surely the most effective of squelches to verbosity."
The Earl of Elgin and Kincardine, K.T.

"*A worthy addition to anyone's library. The exercises are powerful because Philena's been there, got the t-shirt and quit. I read things in this book that made me cry with re-awareness. Re-awareness because we get it, then lose it and have to keep on getting it, until we really GET it in the psyche, body, everywhere. We are loved and the journey is to accept it – this book is a gift.*"
Peta Heskell, Relationship Mentor, www.attractionacademy.com.

"*Philena transmits an important message with inimitable style and humor. She shares what she has learned in life as an expression of love to the world. Love is the message and love is the medium.*"
Martin Brofman, author of *Anything Can Be Healed* and *Improve Your Vision.*

Dedication

In memory of Father Bede Griffiths who gave me unconditional love, total acceptance and started me on my self-healing path.

www.bedegriffiths.com

Foreword

by Leo Rutherford

Healing is a very broad subject and Philena Bruce, in this book, has brought to it a refreshing breeze of common sense and practicality, to say nothing of 30 years of experience. She backs her discourse with lively anecdotes and stories of actual events she has experienced or witnessed. There are numerous ideas which struck home to me in this concise and bullshit-free work.

Firstly, how we view our relationship with the Universe is fundamental to whether healing happens for us. When we hold ourselves as loved by the Universe (God), we hold open the channel for healing and for good vibes of all kinds. If we hold ourselves as sinners struggling for redemption or in any way unlovable and not OK in the eyes of Creation, we block the natural flow. Healing is not so much something done to us as engendered by us so that it can take place within. So how we feel about our self, our worth, our place in the Universe, is fundamental to whether we can let ourselves receive healing or not. Part of the skill of the healer is to get past the client's blocks and create the space where healing can happen.

The feeling of being loved or not is also fundamental to how our life goes and I heartily endorse the practice Philena describes in Chapter 2. We live in a hall of mirrors and the Universe keeps on reflecting our internal thoughts/beliefs to us whether we like what we get or not. And that's the great feedback system of life; we are shown by external events how we are doing in the real world, which is the one inside.

A most useful practice I garnered from this book is the use of symbolic visualization, rather than literal visualization. To replace the scenes of what you want to bring into your life with symbols, thus leaving the Universe greater freedom as to how it brings to you that which you desire. I am currently engaged in working with this method on something that has proved so far to be somewhat intractable in my life. I am expecting success within the next three months!

This brings me to the whole question of materializing what you desire in life, a question which has been highlighted by the popularity of 'The Secret' and other such manuals. There has always seemed to me to be something left out of these theses. I remember a friend back in my San Francisco days who was deeply into this concept and worked her magic on the stock market with spectacular results, until the day when Mr Market had one of his periodic relapses. Her BMW quickly metamorphosed into a beat up Ford Capri and she become sadder but definitely wiser. The Universe gives us what we need, not what we want. Abundance, from a spiritual sense, does not mean ease and plenty in the world of BMW's and McMansions, it means ease and plenty in the world of what really matters: friends, love, a convivial life, compassion and mutual support.

My own journey parallels Philena's in many ways. I, too, grew up in a conventionally mixed up family with blame, shame and guilt thrown around like confetti, and with buckets of judgments regularly put upon me. Thus I learned to judge others in a similar manner and oh so frequently to imagine what awful things they were thinking or saying about me. It took some time in therapy groups to realize that most people were far too busy with themselves to be bothered with judging me, unless I did or said stupid things to bring that about! Turning around and releasing the negative thinking and beliefs taken on in early life is a mega task and Philena gives an excellent series of exercises and meditations which one can do in the little spaces of life, on public transport, while queuing or waiting for something, which help retraining the inner habitual belief system until we grasp our power back.

This is a great manual of commonsense living, healing and helping, read it and find the butterfly within your chrysalis!

Leo Rutherford
www.shamanism.co.uk

Letter to the Reader

Dear Reader,

My own healing path has been a thirty-year-long adventure filled with trial and error. Standing on the edge of sanity trying to find my way to 'normal', I had low self-esteem, felt that no one cared about me and that I was hated by the world. Along the way, particularly in the early years, I discovered many different ways of healing that transformed my life and those of my clients, well beyond my expectations.

I discovered that the vital key to living a happy, fulfilled life was to know that I was unconditionally loved by God, the Universe, the Planet. I know that many people may not be quite ready to take on this belief, as I could not in the early years. Thus you may find it easier to start with one of my other healing methods.

Part I of this book shows you ways to change your life to live in a more fulfilled way. These are methods which anyone can apply with a little perseverance and the desire to live a happier, more successful life. In Part II, I describe the most successful methods of healing which I have practised on myself and my clients, most of which are simple enough to use yourself.

If I were to teach you one thing only, it would be the fundamental truth that **you are unconditionally loved.**

May the Goddess bless you and transform you into the beautiful butterfly you truly are.

Philena Bruce
www.philena.co.uk
www.knowthatyouareloved.com

Acknowledgements

I would like to thank the following people: Angela Clarence for her encouragement, advice, support and endless proofreading; Leo Rutherford for his advice, enthusiasm and his Foreword; Ruth Rankin for keeping various backups of my manuscript on her computer while I was writing this book in India; my sister Eynor Bell, for praying daily that I would have the persistence to write and publish this book, from the moment of its conception until its publication; John Hunt and the rest of the staff of O Books for publishing this book.

I would like to thank Martin Brofman, author of "Anything Can Be Healed" and "Improve Your Vision"; who showed me the awesome power of healing when he cured me of a back problem, chronic food poisoning and total exhaustion, by simply talking to me across a room full of people for 20 minutes about love; and for giving me the courage to believe in my own gift as a healer.

I would also like to thank all my friends and healers who recognized the Goddess within me and without whom I would not have had the strength to keep to my self-healing journey and therefore write this book.

Finally I would like to thank all my clients who trusted me enough to tell me their secrets, and allowed me to help them on their healing path. Without you this book could not have been written.

Note Regarding Names
The names of my clients and friends have been changed to protect their identity, except for Gareth, who has requested that I use his real name. A few minor details have been changed in order to protect the identity of my clients, none of which detract from the authenticity of this book.

Disclaimer

In the case of any emergency, such as an accident, high fever or heart attack, please seek medical attention immediately. If you are worried that you may have a serious illness, please consult a medical professional before trying any of these self-healing techniques.

If you are pregnant, we advise that you seek professional advice before embarking on a self-healing regime.

Neither the author nor the publishers can accept legal responsibility for any problems that may occur when trying the ideas, tips and self-healing techniques in this book.

~

Part I
Methods for Making Your Life
Happier and More Fulfilled

~

Chapter 1

Using Your Mind to Materialize
Your Desires

There are many books written on how to use your mind to get what you want in your life, the most well known being "The Secret" by Rhonda Byrne. Some people have read them all and still fail to get what they want. Some people have read one of them, tried to practise the exercises, not had success and absolutely refuse to read another book on the subject. Some people have had a certain amount of success but when it gets down to what they really want, it does not work. A few people have read one of the books and changed their life beyond all recognition in the next few weeks. Why is this?

I believe that the reason why some people fail with this method is that they do not believe that the Universe loves them, or worse still believe that the Universe hates them. In that case, the Universe is not likely to give you what you ask for, as it would go against your belief system. Often this belief is unconscious rather than conscious, and the beliefs of the unconscious always affect your life more strongly than the beliefs of your conscious. If you want the Universe to provide what you ask for, it is essential that you believe consciously and unconsciously that the Universe loves you. To learn how to do this, see Chapter 2.

You may also have hang-ups on a certain subject, the subject that you are trying to materialize. You may find that you can materialize some things but not others. If for example what you want is very expensive, you may have a belief that you do not deserve good things, in which case your attempts at materialization will fail. You may believe that the Universe only loves you to a certain degree, but it does not love you enough to provide all that you require. Working with a psychotherapist or a healer can often help you to find the cause of your negative beliefs on certain subject matters and help you to remove them. Maybe your parents were poor and always bought second-rate objects leading you to believe that you were not good enough to receive the best. This feeling of not being good enough needs removing.

You may also find that a psychotherapist or healer could be helpful if you are having difficulty persuading yourself to try the various methods of healing that I describe in the other chapters. Often when people cannot persuade themselves to do an exercise which could clearly help them, the reason lies in an unconscious belief that they are wasting their time, or that they do not deserve the result they are hoping for.

The books on how to use your mind to get what you want often suggest you do endless visualizations or other exercises to attain your desires. With the best will in the world this can get boring. I have discovered that the more loved you feel by the Universe, the quicker the result. I have often had a request answered within seconds of asking for it. A desire for something enters my mind, I remember I am loved and that therefore it will be provided. Within the next few minutes what I want either appears or the method for achieving it materializes. It happens again and again and seems completely miraculous. It definitely helps to practise on getting small and everyday desires met, as this builds up your belief system for the bigger things.

Let me give you an example of everyday needs being met. I am writing this book while staying at Shantivanam Ashram in South India. It is very peaceful here and the nearest small town, Kulithalai, is about four kilometres away. Yesterday I felt a great desire to go to Kulithalai for a non-vegetarian meal. The question was how to get there, as it is too far to walk, the buses do not normally stop and it was too late to order a three-wheeler rickshaw. I simply remembered I was loved and knew that a solution would appear. Someone knocked on my door and asked if I would like to go to Kulithalai with him as he had ordered a three-wheeler. Problem solved.

My advice is that when you want something, to first remember that the Universe loves you and then ask for what you want. Feeling loved helps your desire to manifest so quickly, that often it appears before you get round to visualizing it. On the other hand the traditional advice is to decide what you want, visualize yourself as already having it, give thanks for it, then get on with your life, allowing what you have asked for to materialize in its own time.

Another way of going about it is to imagine that the Universe is a loving parent, who absolutely adores you and wants to fulfil your every desire. Ask for what you want, know that the Universe has heard you, and know that your desire will be met.

Are there any dangers? Well when you get good at fast materialization, then you have to be very careful what you ask for. Just make certain you are asking for what you really want. I know somebody who asked to be able to get free of his present job and to be able to do something that was close to his heart instead. He did not mention when he wanted this. Three days later he was sacked from his then present job and two days after that he was offered a job that allowed him to follow his heart. He had hoped the transfer might take place over the next few months, not more or less immediately. After that not only he, but all others who knew of him, became very careful of what they asked for.

My fastest materialization of a large object was when I materialized a piano in eleven hours. I had only done one short visualization on already having it. At the time, I was living with a friend who had space for a piano and I had wanted a piano to practise on. Eleven hours after I had done the visualization someone rang up who was looking for a place to house her piano for a while. I was so shocked at the speed of the materialization that I managed to block the speed of the delivery of the piano, and so had to wait three weeks until it was finally delivered.

Another subject I need to mention is energy. Doing endless visualization exercises to obtain your desires requires energy and you may find you just do not have the energy to do the exercise! Sometimes one feels as if energy only goes out, as if it is just not coming in. I struggled for years to find methods of absorbing energy from the universe other than by sleep. I finally found that the answer is feeling loved. It feeds you. So my advice is put energy into learning to feel loved, after that everything is comparatively easy.

Chapter 2

Remember You Are Loved

Many years ago I thought the world hated me. It was uncanny how badly complete strangers treated me. Then as I taught myself to feel loved, my world changed beyond recognition.

With practice I discovered that when I felt loved, life worked, my needs were met. When things were not going so well, it was always because I had not felt loved for a while.

I discovered that my world is a reflection of me. My energy field defines the world I experience, my emotions define my energy field and how I think defines my emotions. The only thing I have control over is how I think. Thus I taught myself to imagine that I was loved by the Universe. This changed my life.

At the apex of this change in direction many positive things connected to abundance were happening all at once. Bus drivers in London let me on to their buses without a ticket. Black Cab drivers in London would either refuse to take any money saying that they were going that way anyway or they would look at the meter and say, "Just give me a fiver," about half the fare. One London restaurant was feeding me for free, another just asked for half the bill. This second restaurant gave my friends a ten per cent discount even when they turned up without me. I owed £2000 to a shop in Oxford Circus who told me to pay them when I could. They said they trusted me more than the Bank of England. When I took an American friend of mine into my bank to cash travellers cheques, the bank refused to charge commission as she was a friend of mine. Life was just a stream of people wanting to give me things for free, particularly when I needed them.

This state of feeling loved and having my needs met more or

less on demand did not last forever. When I noticed that life was not working, I realized that I had not "felt loved" for a while. So I again began a daily or thrice daily practice of "feeling loved". Having mastered the initial stages of this, I found keeping up the feeling only required the minimum of time. A few times a day I would say to myself, "Remember you are loved" or "I know that I am loved". At the same time I would try to reproduce the feeling. I found this particularly helpful while travelling. When I feel loved, people turn up at the exact moment I need them, whether it is to help me lift a bag, or to help me to get where I'm going.

How to Feel Loved by the Universe

Imagine or pretend that the trees love you, the ones you can see from your home or office or the ones you walk past in the street. Imagine the paving stones love you, the sky, clouds, houses, actually anything that you can see around you which is not human. This is because humans can only give conditional love and you are needing to feel unconditional love. Humans can let you down, trees and paving stones tend not to. You can either spend half an hour a day "feeling loved", or you can do it on the move. Sometimes I would go on special "loving walks" when time was not an issue. As I walked around I would look at things: trees, buildings, paving stones etc and imagine that they loved me.

In the beginning I started with London Underground platforms. I would stand there waiting for a train, imagining the platform loving me. From platforms I progressed to paving stones and trees.

Before I learnt to remember that I am loved, my life was lonely and scary, as it seemed to me that no one cared if I lived or died. At parties or dances no one wanted to talk to me, sit by me or dance with me. I remember family gatherings when 20 or so people would cram into a few cars and drive for miles to a wedding or some other type of party. I would drive alone as no one wanted to go with me, or else a relative would come so as not to feel guilty about my being alone. Doctors told me off for getting ill at weekends. Other doctors would refuse to have me on their lists. People on the tills in shops would shout at me for some imaginary offence. Nobody wanted to go shopping, see a show or go on holiday with me. Life was hell. My family blamed me for bringing unhappiness into my own life. In retrospect, I realize that they were right, I was responsible. I lived a lonely life. I was afraid of people and all sorts of situations. At 29, my misery reached its peak so I left my job and travelled around India for two years.

In South India I met Father Bede Griffiths of Shantivanam Ashram in Tamil Nadu. From him I received as much unconditional love as a human being is capable of giving. This started me on my path of love, though I didn't know it at the time. Father Bede told me that God loved me, or I wouldn't be alive. I didn't believe him. Many years later I decided to believe that God loved me and to teach myself to feel that love, and when I did, it changed my life forever.

Chapter 3

The Magic of Gratitude

Thank You Prayer

I discovered that another way to materialize desires was to give thanks for what I already had, as well as giving thanks for those things I had asked for, as if I already had received them. I developed what I call the "Thank You Prayer". I would sit down in front of my altar, light a candle, and for about 40 minutes thank God for all the good in my life. I would make statements like: "Thank you, God, for my clients who help to finance my life. Thank you, God, for my meals. Thank you, God, for my flat. Thank you, God, for my friends. Thank you, God, for water". At the start I did not think I could keep going for 40 minutes, but as the time went on, I realized I could have kept going for much longer. I found it more powerful and effective to say the statements aloud, rather than in my head.

After that I would ask God for the things I wanted in my life. Then I would thank Him for providing them as if I already had them. I would do this exercise every day for about five days. On day six, many of the things I had asked for would start to appear, and would keep me so occupied that I temporarily forgot about the exercise.

For example, if I needed money in my life, I would spend most of the first 40 minutes thanking God for all the money I had received in the past. I would then ask for more money, followed by thanking God for these new funds, as if I had already received them.

I remember once being very short of money and I practised the "Thank You Prayer" for five days after which numerous clients and therefore money poured into my life, keeping me occupied for months.

A client of mine who was down on his luck and had lost a great deal of money was feeling very sorry for himself. He kept telling me that he only had enough money to buy himself a two-bedroom flat in South Kensington, which is a very sought after and expensive area in London. Most people cannot even afford a bedsit there. I pointed out to him that compared to most people he was very well off. He had never thought of it this way, and that thought alone helped him to feel better. He had been comparing himself to the millionaires of London rather than to the general population.

I find people in the West tend to see what they lack, whereas people in the East tend to see what they have. A Dutch priest who had worked in the missions in Africa told me that when his sister came to visit, he took her to the home of his houseboy who had just got married. She commented to her brother on the hole in his carpet. The houseboy stood in the hole and said, "But look at the lovely carpet I have around the hole!"

This same priest also told me that after the floods some of his parishioners had lost their houses and were asking for him. When he arrived he found one of them sitting fishing on his collapsed house. At the sight of the priest, the man looked at the priest, beamed with joy, and showed him the three fishes he had caught.

You can always find something to thank God for. A side effect of the "Thank You Prayer" is to realize how much better off you are than you thought you were. You can of course thank the Goddess rather than God, or thank the Universe, or the Invisible Power, or any other Being you believe has power over your life. I find that most people acknowledge a power beyond themselves in the Universe, a something that one cannot lay one's finger on; say the "Thank You Prayer" to this Being, you can even call Him/Her, "You Up There" if you like.

One quick word about prayer in general, it does not need to be formal, just talk to a Being beyond yourself from your heart. I was once on a runaway horse, absolutely terrified not knowing what to do next. My prayer at that point was to shout out, "Jesus, do something." The horse slowed down gently, so I was not flung off, and then turned round and trotted slowly back in the opposite direction. A riding school horse galloping for home does not usually stop.

Chapter 4

Don't Judge; Accept Others Just the Way They Are

I have learnt that judging others creates a barrier to the flow of love between them and me. When I accept a person just the way he his, he feels loved by me. This person then accepts me and I feel loved by him. I learnt that feeling loved by another was not connected to whether or not that person loved me, but whether or not that person accepted me.

When I was teaching mathematics to 15-year-olds, one of the girls in my class was very difficult and none of the teachers liked her. I dealt with the girl by ignoring her when she was behaving badly and only responding to her when she treated me with respect. One day I was having a quiet cup of tea when I heard this girl point me out to one of her friends and say, "That's Miss Bruce and she loves me." I was flabbergasted; I could not stand the girl. In retrospect, I realize that I had accepted her the way she was, and thus she felt loved by me.

My basic nature had been to judge everyone, and to judge them as not being okay. This helped me to have very few friends. When I started to accept people just the way they were, all sorts of people started accepting me just the way I was, and as a result we felt loved by each other. When I first realized I had a tendency to judge everyone, I rang a friend of mine and asked him if he did this too. He told me that yes he did, and he judged everything including how the trees blew in the wind and how wide the spaces were between the paving stones in the street. I felt better and thanked God that I had never been that bad!

Learning Not to Judge People I found hard work, as I had to undo a basic part of my nature. I found two exercises, which helped me with this. The first was to look at a person and pretend they had just arrived from Mars, and as I did not know how Martians should behave, I was therefore not in a position to judge the person. The second way was to look at a person and realize that God or the Goddess was inside that person and who was I to judge the Godhead! I used to go out on walks with no other agenda than to look at things and people and not judge them. Thus as I walked down the street, I would look at the rubbish in the street, see it, and not judge it. I found it helped to think of words to describe it which neither denoted good nor bad.

I also discovered through dire necessity how to not feel physical pain. I had an undiagnosed kidney stone and was often in terrible pain. No painkillers had any effect, and no doctor was able to do anything to help. I discovered that if I made a point of feeling the pain and then spoke about it to myself in vocabulary that did not consist of words that meant good or bad, that although I was aware of the pain it did not hurt. I would like to point out that this is something to do in an emergency not instead of visiting a doctor. I finally had the problem diagnosed by a homeopathic doctor in London, just in time to save my kidney.

I remember once speaking to a man in India about not judging pain. He told me he had discovered the same thing with regard to noise. He had lived for many months next to an Indian cinema, blaring out Indian music at full volume on a really bad sound system, 24 hours a day. He learned that by listening to it, but not judging the sound as good or bad, had enabled him to ignore the music, but he was unsure how it might or might not have damaged his eardrums!

Years later, I suffered from downstairs neighbours who played loud music at all hours of the day and night. I had tried screaming at them, threatening them with the police, jumping up and down on the floorboards, trying to have reasonable conversations with them, to no avail. Then I tried listening to it and describing it to myself in words that neither meant good or bad;

for example, it sounds a bit like "spotted yellow". I stopped suffering. Friends or clients would turn up to see me, and say, "How can you tolerate that awful music?" I would say, "What music?" And then realize they were referring to the noise from below which I seemed to no longer hear. I had learnt to accept it.

I successfully used the same method to deal with the cold, when I was stuck in the Himalayas over night with nowhere to sleep and no warm clothes. I felt the feeling on my arms, the goose pimple type feeling, I concentrated hard on it, and described it to myself using non-judgemental vocabulary, such as I feel a type of energy that is vibrating half an inch above the surface of my skin. After a few statements like this, I was no longer conscious of the cold. I have also successfully used the same process when in the tropics and far too hot for comfort.

One way or another I had to put a lot of work and time into my exercises regarding not judging people; either pretending they were from Mars or seeing God or the Goddess in them. This route was successful for me. No longer do I automatically judge people, though I find myself doing it very occasionally, but most times I find myself just accepting people the way they are. I also notice that when I find myself judging someone as not being okay, this is because the person's behaviour is mirroring behaviour which I have not yet dealt with. It is certainly true that the more one accepts oneself and one's own behaviour, the easier it is to accept the behaviour of others. I also learnt that it was very important to include myself when doing non-judgemental exercises.

I know this method works. I have tried it with clients and also read about other people who have changed their own life and the lives of others by applying these basic principles. If you have a colleague at work who is impossible to get on with, someone who is always grumbling or bullying others, is negative or difficult in some other way, try to accept that person just the way he or she is. Do not let your mind use judgemental vocabulary when describing that person to yourself. Do not join in judgemental conversations about that person with another person. Do not judge the person, just wait and see the results. I know of people who have tried this and not only transformed their own relationship with the difficult person, but transformed the relationships in the whole office as a result, turning an office with a difficult atmosphere into a friendly place.

Chapter 5

Tell Yourself Good Lies, Not Bad Ones

Don't Lie to Yourself about the Reasons Behind the Behaviour of Others

I realized that a lot of my misery and the misery of other people is caused by telling ourselves a constant stream of lies. It is so easy to tell oneself that one is not good enough, or that one has fouled up some type of interaction. Or someone else makes a negative comment and one repeats it to oneself 25,000 times over the next few days. I realized at some point that if I was treating another person as badly as I was treating myself, I would probably be in jail! Constantly lying to myself about how hopeless I was led to a miserable, dysfunctional life. I realized that lying to myself in a positive way would help change my life for the better. When I suggested this to clients, they were very resistant to lying to themselves. I pointed out that they were lying to themselves anyway, I was just suggesting they changed the subject matter of the lie, from negative to positive.

I used to put daily effort into telling myself that I was good enough, that I handled interactions well, that I was liked, that I was progressing in life and that I had life much more together than before. After a few weeks, perhaps months, of this "positive lying", I began to see it as truth rather than as a lie.

Like feeling loved and not judging, I found this practice had to be kept up, otherwise I fell back into the old path of negative lying. However, like the exercises of feeling loved and not judging, with time the daily practice shortened and used a lot less energy. I would tell myself good lies as I went about my daily living.

It is also interesting to note that when one constantly lies to oneself, in a negative way, this is judgement of the self. When one judges oneself badly one also tends to judge everyone else badly too. Of course lying to oneself in a positive way is also a form of judgement, however, its effects are positive rather than negative. Also when one judges oneself in a positive way one also tends to judge others in a positive way.

The desire to judge oneself and others negatively comes from how one's parents, teachers, siblings and school friends treated one as a child. Thus it is very important to give your children and other people you love positive comments about themselves and their behaviour.

Another problem I have discovered versus lying is how often people invent reasons behind the behaviour of others; they believe their invention, then blame the person concerned. This is not something I ever went into in a big way personally, but discovered that many people do. Friends and clients of mine often spend many hours each day inventing the reason for another person's behaviour, then believing that invention, then judging that person against their own set of morals. This behaviour can lead to losing friends, clients, and to getting a very unbalanced idea of what actually is going on. I often say to a client, "If you want to know the reason for his behaviour, why don't you ask him, that way you are likely to get near to the truth."

Let me give you an example out of my own life. Many years ago I was spending a six-month stint in Shantivanam Ashram in South India. I had my own hut, and my nearest neighbour was a middle aged German lady, also in her own hut. She and I never spoke; I had it in my head that she did not like me. I was right where that was concerned but wrong as to why. I decided that she did not like me because I smoked in my hut and that was against the rules of the Ashram. I decided she could smell the smoke on the wind, and was angry with me for smoking. At no point, until my last day at the Ashram, did I decide to find out the truth of my assumption. On my last day, I decided to have it out with her. I visited her in her hut, told her I was leaving, and told her that I felt she did not like me. She agreed that she did not like me, but said it was because I wanted her to give me her suitcase. I asked her where she had got that idea from; I had my own suitcases, why would I want hers. She reminded me of a day at the beginning of my stay at the Ashram, when I had passed by her hut, looked inside and said, "Oh what a lovely suitcase you have." I told her that yes I remembered that incident, and it was a nice suitcase, but I did not want it, I had my own. According to her, when people made a nice comment about something you owned it meant they wanted you to give it to them. I made it quite clear that I did not want her suitcase. I mentioned my smoking, she made it clear that she did not know I had been smoking and would not have minded if she had.

This lady and I parted as friends and we both realized how we had stopped a friendship happening because of our faulty ideas about the behaviour of the other. For six months we had lived within 20 yards of each other, and had never spoken, due to both of us believing a lie we each had invented about the other.

Another rather funny example of this concerns my old friend Pablo. Pablo was bankrupt; he went bankrupt quite a few times actually. He had cheated the system one way or another over the years, and eventually had been caught and ended up owing the Inland Revenue more money than he could raise. He had been fairly well off until the Inland Revenue caught up with him and he had to sell most of his properties. He ended up with one falling-down building where he lived, and an ex-shop that was filled with his junk, or antiques, depending on how you looked at it. With the help of friends, and old friends who owed him a thing or two, Pablo managed to feed himself and get by in life.

One day I had a conversation with a local electrician, who

told me that Pablo was really rich and had at least a million hidden somewhere. I tried to tell him that this was not so, but no, he the electrician, knew best, and Pablo was indeed a rich man, pretending to be poor. Some time after this I was out with Pablo when we saw an old bag lady go past. Pablo said, "Just look at her, not a care in the world, now that's a wonderful way to live, she is so happy." I said, "You don't know that, Pablo, she might not be happy." Pablo replied, "I know what I know and that lady is happy. I have an instinct and I know that I'm right." I replied, "You are like the local electrician, he also knows when he is right, and he knows that you have a million pounds hidden somewhere!"

I find that people react in life according to their preconceived patterns; they have been conditioned by their parents and society, and patterns are set that help them get by. We all have different patterns and therefore have different reasons for our behaviour, therefore it is usually impossible to work out another person's reasons for doing or not doing something. So it is not very sensible to start inventing what is going on for another. I find the only sure thing about someone's opinion regarding the behaviour of another is that the opinion will be false!

I had a female client once who went away for the weekend with some girlfriends, just to have an innocent weekend together. Her boyfriend wanted to know where she had gone. She wanted some privacy in her life, so refused to tell him. He decided to believe she had gone to stay with a secret boyfriend. She denied this but would not tell him the truth. This resulted in him dropping her. When she finally told him the truth he was so convinced that his invention was true that he would not listen.

As an adult while staying in my mother's house, if I was late arriving she always assumed that I had had a nasty accident somewhere, or was lying dead in a ditch. My mother, believing her invention, would then have a panic attack, which occasionally led to her ringing up hospitals on my route to see if they had just received any unidentified patients from car accidents, and she would also ring the police to see if they had discovered any unidentified bodies. On the other hand, I had a friend whose parents assumed that she was having a good time somewhere if she was late arriving at their house. So she arrived home to happy parents, I arrived home to a demented mother demanding to know where I had been, why I had taken so long and what I had said to whom.

If you want to be happy in life and would like your loved ones to be happy too, then do not invent reasons for their behaviour, do not lie to yourself about their behaviour, or if you are going to lie to yourself, then at least invent positive reasons not negative ones. With positive reasons, or better still not lying at all, love will flow between you and your loved ones. Negative lies, which are then believed, create immovable barriers, barriers to the flow of love, friendship, companionship, barriers to the flow of life.

Chapter 6

Bless the People in Your Life

Another way I discovered to make my life run smoothly was to spend time each day blessing the people in my life, both those who were now present in my life and those who had been there in the past. I also chose to bless those who would be there in the future. I found this blessing of future people helped calm me about possible future problems. Thus when I was travelling and was unable to lift, let alone carry my suitcase, I blessed in advance all those people who would help me both lift it and carry it. I know suitcases can have wheels, but this does not help on a staircase. I would start a few days in advance and have about two twenty minute sessions a day blessing all those people who would be helping me, then when the time came people would appear just as I needed them. I also felt calm as I approached the time of needing them, because I began to feel their presence in advance.

I also found a good practice, in a blessing session, was to bless the people who had helped me yesterday, bless the people who were helping me today and then bless the people who would be helping me tomorrow.

How to Bless a Person
Say in your mind, "I bless John, I bless the person who helped me carry my suitcase yesterday, I bless the person in the bank who smiled at me today". Imagine sending them a ball of white light, at the same time as saying the words, "I bless so and so". Imagine this ball of light shooting off and surrounding the person.

I used to use this practice before I learnt about feeling loved by the Universe; if you feel loved by the Universe, then your needs will be met, so blessing people is not so necessary where helping yourself is concerned, however, it is nice for the people you are blessing. Also doing something good for another always helps to cleanse your energy field and helps to make you a better receptacle for carrying and producing light and love.

Many years ago, before I learnt about the art of blessing people, I knew a couple who were longing to have a child, but it seemed that the lady concerned was not able to conceive. Her husband was a martial arts teacher and one day he gave me a private lesson. At the end of the lesson he refused to take any money off me. As money was tight for me at that time, I felt an overwhelming sense of gratitude towards him, and in my mind sent a wish that he and his wife would have a child. Two months later his wife confided in me that she was two months pregnant. After the birth of their child, they went on to have triplets on their next attempt! I do not know how much of this was due to my gratitude or how much was coincidence, however, the timing was interesting.

A little while ago a would-be client contacted me and told me he had been cursed over money and asked if I could help. I agreed to see him. I usually find that people who think they have been cursed where money is concerned have actually been very stupid with their money. For example if you give £20,000 in cash to a foreigner you met at the pub three weeks ago to invest in gold shares in Venezuela and you never see the money, the shares or the foreigner again, that is not being cursed where money is concerned, it is not even being unlucky with money, it is crass stupidity. Also, if you took out a bank loan for the £20,000 it may well have turned into £40,000 after 15 years; again this is not bad luck where money is concerned, it is what happens when you take out a loan and fail to pay the interest required on time.

*In this case, the client, let's call him **John**, had parted with a large* *sum of money in £50 notes some 12 years earlier. Having taken out a bank loan, the debt had multiplied over the years, due to John being unable to pay its interest. John had more or less given the money to some bloke he had met at the pub, to buy him a house and had never seen the money, the house or the bloke again. John also told me he thought the man had cursed him as no aspect of his life had worked since he lost the money and he had been in a deep depression for years. His life looked bleak in all directions.*

I gave John a healing session and as far as I could fathom no one had cursed him, other than himself. For 12 years he had been blaming himself for being so stupid and blaming the man who took the money for cheating him. I told John that his £50 notes were somewhere in use in the world. I suggested to John that he visualize his £50 notes and bless the people to whom they now belonged. I suggested John did this for 20 minutes twice a day. Three weeks later John came back to see me, he was a changed man, he was smiling and laughing again, he had lost all his feelings of sadness, anger, rage and guilt over his lost money, and to cap it all his last girlfriend, whom he adored, had contacted him, for the first time in over a year. His friends were telling him that he was a changed man. John told me that it was the blessing exercise which had changed him; as he blessed the people who now had his £50 notes, he had lost all his bad feelings connected to the original incident.

I continued to see John and suggested some practical ways to sort out his financial problems and as a result, he started to see how he could change his life for the better and in time pay off his debt to the bank.

Another way of doing the blessing exercise is to just bless people silently as you meet them, both those who make your day better in one way or another and those who look unhappy and therefore could do with a blessing.

Before I end this chapter, I would like to point out that not everybody who thinks that they have been cursed with regard to money has been stupid. There are genuine cases. See the case of Adriana at the end of Chapter 14 for an example.

Chapter 7

Some Helpful Tips on Communication

I would like to share with you some helpful tips on communication that I have learned over the years.

When Not to Answer the Phone

If you are feeling uptight or irritable do not answer the phone. Answering the phone in the wrong frame of mind is a sure way to lose clients and possibly friends. It is better that a client be annoyed because he cannot get you on the phone than be put off for life because you sounded so irritated.

Dealing with Argumentative People

I have found that when someone is insisting that you agree with their point of view on a subject matter, the answer is to agree, while adding a "but" that is difficult to argue with. For example, when I was in Calcutta in 1980 a friend of mine's uncle was insisting that the poor of Calcutta were basically lazy, that life was easy for them as they had breakfast with the Salvation Army, lunch with Mother Teresa and supper with some other charity. Everyone else in the room was desperately trying to stand up for the poor and getting absolutely nowhere. Then my friend's uncle turned to me and insisted that I agreed with him. I replied, "Yes I agree that the poor are lazy, but you have to remember that most of them have worms and it is well known that one of the side effects of worms is lethargy." This created a tangible silence for a rather long period and then the uncle changed the subject. My friend later told me that never before had anyone successfully shut her uncle up when he was in an argumentative mood.

I once witnessed something similar in my flat, when a group of us were about to go out to a pre-planned meal at a restaurant. Suddenly one member of the group said belligerently she had grievances she wanted to air, and that she wanted to air them then and there on the spot and wanted us all to discuss them. A friend of mine, who was an assertiveness trainer, took control of the situation. She agreed that this lady's grievances were important and needed to be discussed, and asked us all to take out our diaries so we could arrange a date for this. This way we got to our restaurant on time, and the person with the grievances was not in a position to continue insisting that we had the discussion then and there.

Standing Up For Yourself

I have had plenty of experience with people who like to put you down and make you feel small. This happened a great deal in my family who seemed to think that if they put you down, it made them okay. I find the opposite to be true. If you praise another person, you actually go up in their estimation.

I grew up with very low self-esteem due to being constantly put down by my family as well as by teachers and other children at school. I finally learnt that to get my self-esteem back I had to stand up for myself the moment I was put down. And to be prepared to do this whenever and wherever it happened. I also learnt that it is very important not to put the other person down as this just starts a slanging match. By doing this I found I could change the behaviour of another person towards me in a very short period of time. It also meant that I became used to being treated better with a consequent rise in my self-esteem. Let me give you a couple of examples.

I was to be left alone with one of my male relatives for a week. I dreaded this as I had been afraid of him all my life. He was one of the most arrogant members of my family and was first class at putting people down. I decided that I would stand up for myself, come what may. The first evening after supper, I was faced with a row of buckets to put the food I had not eaten into; there was the chicken bucket, the pig bucket, the goat bucket, the compost bucket and the rubbish bin. Not being knowledgeable on the subject of chicken, pig and goat food, I asked which bucket I should put what in. The reply I got was, "Oh for goodness sake, Philena, just use your brain." It was said as if I was the stupidest person on the planet. I stood up for myself wanting to say something like, "There is no need to speak to me that way, there is absolutely no reason why I should automatically know which buckets to use." But as I was unused to standing up for myself, it came out as gibberish but the message got through. The next day I had to stand up for myself again but this time I was able to do it in plain English. To this day, I have had no more trouble with that relative.

One Easter Sunday I was at a family luncheon with thirty people present. During a conversation I made a comment to which one of my relatives said something like, "Oh don't be so ridiculous, Philena." The words may sound alright as you read them now, but at the time the lady's tone was extremely condescending. I just said loudly, "Please repeat that." A few people looked up. Of course the person concerned did not want to repeat it, so silence prevailed. Again I asked loudly for a repeat of what she had said. Slowly the whole table started looking at the person concerned and asked her to repeat it, she sounded very silly, finally mumbling that she had forgotten what she had said. I have never been treated badly again by her, or by any of the other people at that table. They all got the message that they needed to treat me with respect. People do not like being confronted, particularly in public.

Standing up for oneself can be daunting for those not used to it. Standing up for oneself with one person is bad enough, doing it in front of a group can be terrifying. However, it is only terrifying the first time, the second time is easier and the third time is almost easy and from then on it probably won't be necessary, or if it is, it becomes really easy. What is not obvious here is that when you don't stand up for yourself it somehow gets written in your energy field and complete strangers instinctively pick up on the fact that they can bully you. Once you learn to stand up for yourself the information in your energy field changes and strangers are far less likely to attack you.

Learning to Stand Up for Yourself is just a matter of doing it. Once you have done it, it is learned. Even if you do it in gibberish on your first attempt, it can still work. The thing not to do is attack the other person. It does mean living your life consciously, responding immediately to any insulting behaviour. It is no use attempting to stand up for yourself a few hours after the incident.

You can let people walk all over you for the rest of your life, or the next time someone tries to put you down you can stand up for yourself. You just have to make a commitment to do it.

Dealing with Jealous People

I have found that other than being born, you do not need to do anything in particular for people to be jealous of you. When I was born, I had four older sisters and all of them were jealous of me. I was only aware that in their eyes I was not "good enough". So any time I achieved something which might make me "good enough", it only served to increase their jealousy. Added to which my mother apparently boasted about me non-stop, although she rarely said anything nice to my face.

When someone is jealous of you, do not tell them good things that are happening in your life, otherwise they will become even more jealous. On the other hand when bad things are happening in your life, tell that jealous person, as this is likely to reduce their jealousy.

Can jealous people damage you, or is it just that it makes you feel bad and makes for a difficult relationship? From experience, I would say that yes, jealous people can damage you, because they are sending you negative thoughts and emotions. And whether done consciously or unconsciously, this is a form of psychic attack and the results are just as harmful, regardless of whether the perpetrators are aware of it or not.

To see how to release yourself from psychic attack see Chapter 14.

Sorting Out a Relationship Problem when both sides would ideally like the relationship to work

Find a three to four hour slot when neither of you are tired, and a place where you can't be interrupted by telephones, doorbells or children. Decide who is going to start; tossing a coin is often helpful for this. The first person talks non-stop about their side of the problem, concentrating on how they feel and not using blame vocabulary. The other person sits and listens, does not take notes and does not interrupt in any way. The first person talks until they feel finished, which usually takes about an hour. Then the second person talks while the first person listens, which tends to take another hour. This is followed by a second and possibly third round. In many cases, a referee can be helpful to monitor blame vocabulary on the part of the speaker and to make sure that the listener does not interrupt.

By blame vocabulary I mean that it's not okay to say, "When you do such and such *you make me* angry". Instead say something like, "When you do such and such, I feel hurt, let down, not wanted and then I find myself getting angry to protect myself". In other words don't blame the other person for how you react, thus taking responsibility for your own reactions.

The reason that this method is so successful is because as the listening person cannot interrupt, take notes or otherwise amuse themselves, they end up really listening, giving them a chance to really understand what is going on for the speaker, possibly for the first time. Very few relationship problems need more than one of these types of sessions.

I practise this method with clients who want to sort out their relationship problems, taking the part of the referee, and find that this method tends to get very good results. .

Protecting Yourself from the Sound of Drilling

If you live in a town you may suffer from days of being driven mad by having to listen to the sound of workmen drilling in the road outside your home. This happens a lot where I live and many years ago I discovered an unusual way of dealing with it.

Put a mirror on your windowsill or in your garden so that it faces the direction of the drilling. This protects you from the energetic impact of the sound. If you are trying to meditate at the time, the difference with the mirror in place should be noticeable to you. And with time you may find that the presence of your mirror somehow brings the drilling to a halt.

I have a small mirror framed in bamboo that I put outside my windows at the first sound of drilling. Nine times out of ten, the drilling stops immediately my mirror is in place. Over the years many of my clients have witnessed this happening. I remember once stopping a session I was doing with a client to put the mirror outside. I told her what I was about to do and my client reacted as if I was mad. As I put the mirror down, the drilling ground to a halt. "You see it works," I said. The client replied, "It will start again." Two hours later as my client left, I said to her, "Did you notice that the drilling did not start again!"

~

Part II
Successful Methods of Healing I Have Used Over the Last 20 Years

~

Chapter 8

Symbolic Visualization

In my early days of healing, I learnt how very effective Symbolic Visualization could be for bringing about change. In the late eighties much was spoken about how to attract what you want in life through visualization. However, it was very important that you visualized all the little details otherwise something could go wrong. There were stories about people who visualized owning Rolls Royces, but due to not visualizing correctly they received them in peculiar ways. One man was visualizing having a Rolls Royce, but it careered off the road and came through his sitting room wall! (Whether this story is true or not, I do not know.) However, I do know someone who visualized owning a deep freeze, but didn't visualize the colour. It came in lime green, the ugliest deep freeze anyone had ever seen. The same person visualized getting a flat but forgot to include where she wanted it. She got one in Birmingham, rather than in London where she wanted to live. A friend of mine told me about a woman who visualized a male lover in every tiny detail she could think of. He was everything she had asked for, but had foul breath!

I discovered that Symbolic Visualization is a way of avoiding the pitfalls that go with normal visualization.

The essence of a successful Symbolic Visualization is to find the right symbol to explain your present situation. You then adjust it until it feels right or complete. To find the right symbol you need to relax and allow your subconscious to show you a picture. To look for it consciously is a complete waste of time. Also a symbol that works for one person is not likely to work for another; you need to find the symbol that relates to you at this moment in time.

Let me share with you a Symbolic Visualization that I did many years ago, which completely cured my friend's mother's back problem.

*I was at my friend **Frances's** birthday party and I learnt that her mother had a back problem. She had been to an osteopath a few times but the pain kept returning. While we were waiting for pudding I sat behind her, put my hands on the part of her back that hurt, felt the heat coming from it, then asked in my mind for a picture. I saw a long soggy sausage hanging between two rusty hooks. I realized I needed a new sausage and new stainless steel hooks, so I called up a van, with two men, who brought me a brand new sausage and two new stainless steel hooks. In my mind, I held on to one end of the soggy sausage, removed the rusty hook, cleaned out the hole with white light, put in a new hook, then hung one end of the new sausage on the new hook. Then I did the same process at the other end of the soggy sausage, leaving the brand new sausage hanging on the new hooks. I threw away the old sausage and rusty hooks and clicked my fingers to dematerialise them; which is a way of getting rid of psychic debris. Once I was finished, the heat coming from her back was replaced by what I considered to be a normal energy feel. I then asked her how she felt. She said, "Just before you opened your mouth, the pain went." The whole visualization had taken just ten minutes.*

I was in touch with Frances's mother for a few weeks after this, and am still in touch with her today. The pain never came back.

Some years ago, my cash flow was heading for a crisis with more going out than was coming in and I was nearing the bottom of my overdraft facility. I was facing rising panic. One night around 2 a.m. I decided to see what I could do about the situation. I relaxed and tuned into how I felt. I realized I felt as if I was in an oxygen tent and the pipe supplying the oxygen was getting smaller and smaller. So I made the pipe bigger, as big as the waste pipe from a lavatory. Then I decided to add some more oxygen pipes, of similar size. I ended up with four of them. About seven hours later, at 9 a.m., an increased flow of clients and money began to pour into my life. This went on for weeks, if not for months.

So first visualize your problem symbolically. Your subconscious will help you. When you have found the right symbol enter into it fully. Use all your senses: sight, hearing, taste, smell and touch. What does it feel like? What do you feel emotionally? Adjust the picture to one that feels good. Use your senses again and notice the difference.

Over the years I have practised Symbolic Visualization with many of my clients, often with phenomenal results. On various occasions we added a date to the visualization, and it has been amazing how many people's results turned up on that exact date. Here are a few examples of the success some of my clients have had with this method.

David had been a rich man, but due to a burglary and a problem with his insurance, he found himself owing the bank a million pounds. I suggested to David that we did a Symbolic Visualization to sort out his finances. As David was a businessman used to left brain thinking, he found doing a Symbolic Visualization using his right brain rather hard, but he came up with an apple tree that would not let him pick the apples. I suggested he asked the tree when he would be able to pick the apples, the tree replied that he could pick them when they were ripe. I told him to ask the tree for the date when the apples would be ripe. A date was given nine months in advance. I wrote the date in my diary and asked David to write it in his, I also told him to practise the visualization at least once a day but David was a very busy man and actually managed to only do the visualization about twice a week.

The bank made an appointment with David to discuss his debts the very day the apples were due to become ripe. But the day before

David rang me in a state of great upset. Someone had bashed into his parked car, had not left any details, and he only had third party insurance. David had sold most of his properties to pay back the bank. His car, one of his remaining assets, was very close to his heart. The only thing I could think of saying to him was to get his priorities right, never mind the car, he must concentrate on the interview with the bank.

What happened at the bank the next day was very interesting. David arrived looking awful and terribly sad as he could not get his ruined car out of his head. David was normally a rather arrogant man. The bank had never seen him looking so upset and assumed he was upset about the money that he still owed, around half a million pounds. They wrote off the remainder of his debt which allowed him to keep his car and one small property to live in. And this happened on the exact day given in the Symbolic Visualization nine months earlier.

Susannah *was a lady with many emotional problems. Her husband had decided to divorce her. Knowing Susannah, one could not help but feel sympathy for the husband. Susannah had great difficulty focusing on anything, however, the upcoming divorce enabled her to concentrate better than she ever had before. There were also children involved. Susannah did a Symbolic Visualization to keep her family together. The image she chose was a family picnic at the bottom of the ocean, together with an elephant. I do not think we put an exact date on this, just an approximation as to time of year. I sent Susannah away to practise this visualization. Around the time that Susannah's visualization was going to come to fruition, I received a card from her telling me that her husband had changed his mind and they had got back together and were blissfully happy.*

Nancy *desperately wanted a husband. We first did some healing to clear up past relationships. Then Nancy chose to do a Symbolic Visualization to get her man. While I don't remember the symbol she came up with, we put a date on the visualization for about six* *months in the future, and either the day after that date, or the day before, Nancy married the man of her dreams. It is now many years later and they are still happily married.*

Jo had problems in every area of his life, particularly in his relationship and his career. He had to find a new job as his present firm was shutting down. He was a city man, where finding new jobs normally takes months of hard work. I suggested a Symbolic Visualization. I cannot remember the exact subject of Jo's symbol, but it was something to do with a field and a horse. A week after we did the Symbolic Visualization a possible job had materialized. Four weeks later Jo was happily established in this job and he and his wife were getting on so well, that his wife told me that they had never had it so good.

Bankers, lawyers and business people, particularly if they are male, find it very hard to let go of their left brains. On the other hand children, dreamers and artists tend to be much more in contact with their right brains. Symbolic Visualization together with many other sorts of healing needs to be done with the right brain. I have discovered that children, gay people and women who are not connected with the financial sector, find this type of work fairly easy. People from the financial sector and straight men find it more difficult, but not impossible.

In case you have not heard of the terms left brain and right brain, let me explain. The left brain is to do with logical thinking, understanding words and music. The right brain is to do with pictures, dreaming and art. The unconscious works through the right brain.

Now you might ask me if all the Symbolic Visualizations I have done with clients have been successful. The truthful answer to this is that I do not know, but over a 20 year period of practising these visualizations with clients, only one has contacted me to say that it did not work. On the other hand many have contacted me to relate their successes.

There are two types of problems that can stop a visualization from working. One is when the person fails to practise it. The other is when the person forgets their visualization is symbolic. The one failure I am aware of fits the latter category. The lady concerned came from South America. She wanted to solve her money problems. She chose for her symbol a picture of watching her boats come in. Interestingly she did not know that "your boats coming in" is an English expression for getting rich. She practised her visualization religiously, together with an exact date. However, she forgot it was symbolic and forgot that they were supposed to be "her" boats coming in. Her job sent her to Malta over the date when her boats were due in. On the exact date she was in Malta harbour watching boats coming in. So in one way her visualization was a success but regarding her finances it was a failure.

It is easy enough to remember that your visualization is symbolic if you are having a ride on a flying elephant, or a picnic at the bottom of the sea, but if your symbol is possible on this planet, then you have to remember to remind yourself that it is only symbolic of whatever it is that you want to achieve.

How to Create a Symbolic Visualization

Decide what it is that you really want. Be precise. Get your desire clear in your mind before you start. Do not think of something you think you would like, like winning the lottery, but something that you really need in your life. Choose something that can be easily defined, and which has feelings attached.

Sit in a comfortable chair with your feet flat on the floor, shut your eyes, and relax your whole body. One way is to start at the top of your head, and imagine it relaxing, and then go down your body, part by part, imagining each part relaxing. For example, relax your head, your eyes, your nose, your ears, your mouth and your jaw muscles; they are just under your ear lobes. Relax your neck, your shoulders, your back and your chest. Relax your arms, your hands and your fingers. Relax your stomach, your pelvic area, your thighs, the tops of your legs, your knees, the bottoms of your legs, your calf muscles, your ankles, your feet and your toes. Then re-check the three areas where most people hold tension; that is your jaw muscles, your shoulders and your thighs. Re-check any area where you know that you personally tend to hold tension.

Relax your mind, and then let your problem, with all its emotions and feelings, wash over you. Allow a picture to appear in your mind which describes your problem. For example you may feel that you are stuck in a room with no windows or doors, or you may feel that you are stuck in a type of bubble floating in space, or that you are in the desert and all you can see around you is sand, or you may be on a desert island all by yourself, or at sea in a boat which is going round in circles, or thigh deep in mud, or stuck at the bottom of a well, or in a forest where everything feels unfriendly. You may also feel that you are a damaged rose in a garden of healthy roses, or a lost bird. Just see which image floats into your mind.

Once you have found your image, get into the picture, notice what you can see, hear, smell, touch and taste. You should not be able to see your face. If you can it means that you are looking at yourself from a distance, in which case you need to re-enter your body. Perhaps you can touch something in your picture and feel its texture, maybe there is something you can taste. If relevant, notice what type of day it is and what you are wearing. Notice how you are feeling emotionally. Then change your picture until you become content with the surroundings. In your picture you are all powerful, you can do anything that you can imagine. You can fly through the air, use laser beams, summon up people or angels to help you. For example, if you are in a boat going round in circles you can take control of the boat, order up a good wind, find yourself sailing to a land where the sun shines and the grass is green. You can then get out of your boat and walk around this new land, and maybe find yourself a nice house, or just enjoy sitting on the grass. If you are stuck in mud, you can create a plank of wood to help you walk to solid ground, or imagine a wind or the sun drying up the mud, or a balloon coming and rescuing you and taking you to solid ground. If stuck at the bottom of a well, you may see a staircase out, or you can call upon angelic assistance or maybe you can call out and someone will hear you and help you.

Having changed your picture to one that feels good, then again notice what you can see, hear, smell, touch, and, if relevant taste. Notice how you feel emotionally. Then allow yourself to know which year it is, which month it is, and maybe which day it is. If the date is far later than you want, do not change it. Maybe the time between now and your final scene will take a couple of years, however, your life will improve steadily between now and that time.

How to Practise your Symbolic Visualization

Sit down, close your eyes, relax your body. Take a few minutes over this, you must be properly relaxed before you start. Then remind yourself that you are doing a Symbolic Visualization to bring into your life whatever it is that you have chosen. Repeat the visualization that you did before, make it exactly the same as it was the first time. Remember to use your senses at the beginning and at the end, and maybe during it as well, if relevant. By your senses I mean notice what you can see, hear, smell, touch and taste. Also notice what you feel emotionally. At the end, remind yourself of the date and then remind yourself again that this is a Symbolic Visualization to bring into your life that which you have chosen. Then get up and get on with your life.

Do not think about your visualization all day, this can stop it from working. Your visualization is like aiming an arrow at a target, for the arrow to reach the target, you must let go with the bow. Therefore when you have finished practising your visualization it is important that you occupy your mind with something else.

I usually suggest that people practise their visualization between one and three times a day. If you do one before you go to sleep, then sit up in bed and do it, so you do not go to sleep in the middle. First thing in the morning is a good time, as your body will be relaxed. Practise for six weeks or until your goal manifests in your life, whichever comes sooner. You can practise it for more than six weeks, but you are likely to get bored. In the beginning it is likely to take 15 or 20 minutes, but after awhile you could get it down to five minutes.

If your visualization has more than two scenes in it, then after a few weeks you may find that the beginning of your visualization is no longer relevant as you have now left behind that bit of your life. If this is the case, then start your visualization at say the second scene in it, or from wherever you now feel is relevant.

Always use your senses and your emotions. Your senses set the scene. Your emotions are the magic which makes it work.

A Word on Good Practice for Symbolic Visualization

Do not use Symbolic Visualization to change the life of another person without their permission. Do not use Symbolic Visualization to obtain something which belongs to another. Most important of all do not use Symbolic Visualization to cause harm to anyone. For example it is okay to use it to find a husband but not to persuade John Brown to marry you, it is okay to use it to get a Rolls Royce, but not to ask for John Brown's Rolls Royce. If you use it in ways which are not alright, you are likely to attract a negative payback into your own life. I know of people who have used various powers to change others without their permission, I also know of what happened to those people later and it was not pretty. For example a client of mine was very angry with her boyfriend, who was seeing other women behind her back, so she used her mind to make him lose his job. He lost his job then left her. She was eight and a half months pregnant with his child, without money or friends, a foreigner alone in the UK.

Another of my clients used her mind to make a certain man marry her; she told me she suffered for ten years as a result and now realizes that it was a very stupid thing to do.

If you are furious with someone and can only think of revenge, then I suggest you do a Relationship Healing with that person, see Chapter 9, and get the anger and pain out of your system, that way you do not run the risk of damaging yourself. When you use your energy to produce love, love lives in your energy field attracting good things to you, when you use your energy to produce hate, hate lives in your energy field attracting bad things to you. If a person has damaged you as a result of their behaviour, do not damage yourself even more by sending bad energy to that person. Release your feelings towards that person and move on with your life. It may be difficult at this point, but try to remember that YOU ARE LOVED.

Chapter 9

Relationship Healings

Early on in my healing career I developed a Relationship Healing. So many people are in pain over a failed loving relationship, or a bad relationship with a parent, that their lives are only partially operational. I found that people were not only holding on to their own pain, but that of the other person as well. Free that pain and both the client and the other person will regain energy and a greater enjoyment of life. Following a session people have rung to tell me how different, or how much more reasonable, their father, mother or lover has become. I also see a marked physical change in my clients' appearance; they seem healthier and more alive, so much so that I often think I should take before and after photos!

How I do a Relationship Healing with a Client

In a healing session I ask the client to sit in a comfortable position with his feet flat on the ground, his hands on his lap but not touching each other and his eyes shut. I then ask him to go in his mind to a place where he feels safe, preferably in nature, like in a wood, in a garden or on a beach; to see and really feel where he is, noticing sights, sounds and smells. I ask the client to see walking towards him the person with whom he would like to do a Relationship Healing. I suggest that both of them sit down somewhere comfortable. I ask the client to ask the other person if he/she is willing to sort out their relationship. Having received a "yes", I ask the client to talk to the other person, saying everything he needs or wants to say about their relationship and what has happened or is happening in it. I encourage the client to release his pain, anger, guilt, whichever negative emotions are relevant. When the client has finished I ask him to pretend to be the other person and to talk back to himself. After the other person has finished, I ask the client to switch back to being himself and to talk to the other person again. I allow each person to speak three times. This way the client releases his own pain as well as the pain of the other person, which he is carrying.

Although it is possible to do a Relationship Healing on oneself, I do not recommend it. For the Relationship Healing to be successful your pain needs to be "heard". I have discovered that when a person's pain is "heard" the pain then goes. It is the healer's job to "hear" that pain. A healer can only "hear" your pain if he or she has been through similar pain "and" had it healed. Also a good healer can tell when you have finished and be there for you energetically should you become very emotional, which often happens in successful Relationship Healings. I find that most clients think they have finished long before they actually have; I need to give them lots of encouragement to keep going, often by telling them to repeat the same thing over and over again when they cannot think of anything different to say. A client is not finished until all the relevant emotions have been felt and released, at which point taking on the role of the other person is fairly simple. I can tell with my hands from the feeling of the client's energy field when he has finished.

Later on I developed Toning, a sound made with the human voice, which releases emotions far more quickly than talking does. When I first introduced Toning to my healing sessions, I reduced my session times from about four hours to three hours. So now my Relationship Healing sessions consist of a mixture of talking and Toning. For more information on Toning see Chapter 10.

Let me give you some examples of successful Relationship Healings.

Chloe was hopelessly in love with one of the numerous Mr Wrongs.

It was obvious to me that Chloe was attached to a person who could not bring her happiness. Chloe's man had decided to end the relationship first; he wanted to get out quickly, to avoid Chloe hurting him at a later date. Chloe was devastated and could not get the man to see sense. At the time Chloe was about 20, she arrived for a session looking more like 80, her life was not functioning at all, and she was on sick leave from work. During the session, Chloe released all her pain and frustration over the situation; she also released the man's fear of relationships not working out. At the end of the session Chloe looked like a carefree 20-year-old. She left me saying that she was not going to let her man ruin a potentially good relationship and she would deal with the situation. My heart sank, as I felt their relationship had no future.

Chloe returned a couple of weeks later to do a Relationship Healing with her father. I asked her how it had gone with the boyfriend. She told me she had met him in a restaurant and had spent some time trying to get him to see that it was stupid ending a relationship in case it went wrong at a future date. Then suddenly she realized she was wasting her time, and he was not worth it, so she got up and walked out and left him to pay the bill. She had not thought of him since.

A few years later Chloe rang to tell me she was now married to a wonderful man, had just had a baby, and was ringing to thank me for rescuing her from the wrong relationship so many years back.

Mary *came to me to do a Relationship Healing with her problematic sister. She arrived announcing that she was not angry with her sister, all the other therapists she had been to had told her she was angry with this sister, but no she was not. I told Mary that if she thought she was not angry with her sister, well she was probably right. From experience I have found that clients usually know their situation better than anyone else.*

During the Relationship Healing, as soon as Mary pretended to be her sister, the anger poured out. Mary learnt why her sister was angry with her, why the relationship between them was not working. Mary left me knowing what it was she was doing in their relationship that made it so bad. Over the next few weeks, Mary treated her sister very differently, as she now understood more about how her sister ticked. After two or three months, Mary's relationship with her sister improved so much that they started to have a very good relationship. The interesting thing here is that Mary was indeed carrying anger connected to her sister, but it was her sister's anger, not Mary's, that is what the other therapists had got wrong.

James *had an appalling relationship with his father, however, as his father was a rich man and James was always penniless, James needed a decent relationship with his father so he could continue to be bailed out when necessary. James seemed unable to work and was suffering from depression. This is very common amongst rich people's children; the parents feel guilty for one reason or another and bail out their children so they can live fairly well-off lives. When you have someone giving you money whenever you need it, earning a living is much less attractive. James, on the few occasions he had got a job, had never stayed there for longer than a week, often he would leave after the first day.*

I remember James's Relationship Healing with his father well, anger poured out in copious amounts from both sides. James managed to bounce up and down on his knees on a mattress yelling out his fury at his father for 30 minutes before he showed any signs of getting tired. By the end of the healing, James was peaceful and exhausted. A couple of weeks later he spent Easter with his father and according to the message he left on my answer phone, it was the best time that they had had together since James had been a small boy.

I did many other Relationship Healings with James and his various relatives. He stopped coming to see me after awhile, so I did not get round to helping him solve his work issues, however, healing the relationships within his immediate family enabled James to recover from his depression.

A Relationship Healing with someone who has died is usually far easier than when the person is still alive. I believe this is because the soul of the dead person turns up and helps with the healing. This is a great help to people who have lost a loved one, particularly those who did not have a chance to say goodbye.

Rachel could not come to terms with the death of her mother, who had suddenly been killed by a terrorist bomb. During her Relationship Healing, Rachel kept asking her mother why she had gone to that place on that day, why she chose to die. When Rachel became her mother, she said that she had enjoyed her death as it had enabled her to get all over the papers, "You know how I like to get into the press, darling." I was a little worried at this point, as I was wondering what effect this would have on Rachel, but by the end of the healing, Rachel was at peace about her mother's death. She told me that it now made sense, her mother had always adored being in the press! I spoke again to Rachel some months later and she was well and was getting on with her life, now that she was able to put her mother's death behind her.

Clara came to see me to do a Relationship Healing with her grandmother who had died before Clara had had time to say goodbye. Clara had hopped on an aeroplane to see her dying grandmother, but did not arrive in time. Clara had been devastated ever since. The Relationship Healing went very well and during it, Clara was able to see and feel the presence of her grandmother in a vision. In this case I did not need to get Clara to pretend to be her grandmother as she could hear her grandmother's voice. Clara just repeated to me what her grandmother was saying. Later Clara told me that it was the most amazing experience of her life. She was aware of lying on my sitting room floor, but at the same time she was miles away with her grandmother, really seeing her as if she was still alive.

Over the years, various people have reported similar experiences to Clara's; that is they had a vision of the person who had died, could hear their voice and in some cases even feel their touch. One lady came many times, and she had a vision every time. I asked her if she had experiences like this at home, and she said no. She said she would not be paying to see me if she could have these visions without me! Most of the people who have visions seem to be gay men or are female, all of them are sensitive souls.

Many people who come to see me for a Relationship Healing are heartbroken because their partner has left them. As a result of the healing they are able to finally let go of their pain and get on with their lives. However, a few people prefer to continue to hang on to their pain, they do not want to let go, they are not open to meeting another person at a later date, they just want Mr or Mrs Wrong back, they are very obsessive over the situation, and there is little that anyone can do to help them. You have to want to get better to be helped. If you do not want to get better, then it is a waste of time and money to have a healing. Some people have actually said that they want to hang on to their anger, maybe forever.

A Relationship Healing is also very helpful for those in a loving relationship which is going badly. By the end of the session the client has released all of their negative emotions, has had the opportunity to say everything that they want to say to their partner, as well as receiving some input as to where the partner is coming from. This enables the client to go home and have a useful conversation with their partner as to what is going on in their relationship. As the client has released their emotions on the subject, if during the conversation their partner gets into blame mode, the client is able to handle it, rather than having a need to shout back, this in itself is very healing for the partner. I find that people get better emotionally after they have been heard. I hear the client, then the client goes home and is able to hear what their partner needs to say, then a healing can take place between them.

*Let me give you an example of a whole family being healed after one of them did a Relationship Healing. When **Lillie** was two, she hated her baby sister. Then her baby sister died. Lillie's parents did not have the counselling they needed. They chose to deal with the situation by never talking about their dead daughter. Lillie felt guilty as she thought her hatred of her sister had killed her. So Lillie grew up feeling guilty; never having the opportunity to talk about her guilt or her sister, it was like a heavy blanket over the family. No one dared talk about it.*

We did a Relationship Healing with her sister who had died. Lillie released her guilt and was able to totally accept that she had not been the cause of her sister's death. It was quite clear from the healing that the baby who had died was happy now and her soul made it clear that she was only meant to have had a short earth life, everything was the way it was supposed to have been. Lillie was transformed and glowed with health. A couple of weeks later, Lillie went to visit her parents and had the opportunity to speak to her mother about her dead sister. Lillie was able to provide the space for her mother's pain to be released, her mother cried and cried and finally looked revitalized. A few days after this, Lillie's mother rang her to say that she had had a conversation about the dead child with her husband, and as Lillie's mother had released her own pain, she was able to be there for her husband, so he was also able to cry his heart out. Thus Lillie's family were healed.

Lillie felt at peace with the world, although her numerous problems in life were still very much there. Lillie had the feeling that everything was alright, although looking at Lillie's life it looked as if nothing was alright. Then after about four weeks, Lillie's life changed more or less overnight. Her mother paid off all her debts. Her boyfriend asked her to marry him. They found and bought an ideal home in Spain where Lillie found a job close to the house. From that moment on, Lillie's life went forward on a different footing, a much better footing.

You may be wondering why Relationship Healings work, whereas crying your heart out at home does not, nor does talking to your friends, though it may help a little. The secret lies in talking "to" the person, rather than "about" the person. And the pain needs to be "heard." As the healer, I hear the client's pain. Hearing is not the same as listening. The client's pain needs to be heard by one who has been through that pain and had it healed. For most people when they start to listen to a person's pain it brings up their own unhealed pain and they unconsciously stop the healing from taking place.

Over the years I have done successful Relationship Healings in numerous languages, most of which I cannot speak or understand. I remember once saying to a client, it does not matter which words you use. It is your feelings I need to hear, if you like you can say, "Rhubarb, rhubarb, rhubarb". "If you don't mind, I'd rather talk," said the client!

A change in the client's voice when pretending to be the other person is very common, though usually the client is unaware of it. It shows me that the client is deep into the healing, and it is a very positive sign for a successful outcome.

I would like to make clear that when the client releases the pain of the person they are doing the Relationship Healing with, they only release the pain to the extent that they themselves are holding on to it. Thus when Chloe released her boyfriend's fear of relationships ending, she released that of his fear that she herself was holding. For her boyfriend, his fear of relationships ending was still there. The way I understand it, is that when you love someone you absorb some of their pain, anger, fear etc. This pain, anger, fear that you have absorbed needs releasing, as it does not belong to you and a way to release those emotions is through pretending to be that other person.

Regarding the change to the other person I assume that this is brought about by the client's changed attitude to that person. The client treats them differently. Therefore their boyfriend or parent behaves differently towards the client. The client acts more positively, and so their friend or parent acts more positively. It looks as if the friend or relative has changed, whereas it is the client who has changed and therefore the relationship changes.

Most Relationship Healings are successful and most people only need to do one session to heal their relationship, unless the person is doing a Relationship Healing with their mother. In this situation, one session is hardly ever enough. Why mothers need more than one session I'm not sure, it may be because I, personally, had a very difficult relationship with my mother that took far longer to heal than my relationships with other people.

The following situations can stop a Relationship Healing from working: when the client refuses to do what I ask him to do, when a client is unable to let go and let happen what wants to happen, when a client insists, consciously or unconsciously, to be in control of the healing, when a client's anxiety as to what might happen overrides his desire to get better, when a client does not really want to heal the relationship concerned, but is having the healing to satisfy someone else's demands. There are also some people who like to visit all the therapists and healers around and to prove that what they do does not work.

I would like to say a word or two about anxiety. Over the years, various clients have come to me and said something like, "I know what you do has worked for all my friends, but I don't think it will work for me." At that point I know that it will work for the person concerned, because he has just released his fear that it will not, by voicing it to me. Other clients are anxious about the process as they have not done anything like this before, and they do not know me very well. In this case, their first session is getting to know me better, and learning about how I work. On their second session, they usually let go, and the healing takes place.

There are also anxiety disorders, including different forms of OCD (Obsessive Compulsive Disorder), which fit a different category. These clients have so many questions that there is no time left for the healing. A few brave souls keep coming back till they have had all their questions answered quite a few times, and then they are prepared to let go and let the healing take place. I find Toning very helpful in these situations, as it allows the client to find the source of his anxiety and then to let it go. From my experience OCD can be healed, but it can take many sessions, and the client needs to be prepared to enter his fear during the healing as it has to be felt before it can be released.

A Word on Forgiveness

Many people talk today about the importance of forgiveness: that you will never be free, happy or healthy unless you learn to forgive.

I have found with my clients and myself, that it is impossible to forgive if you have not had your pain heard. You can say that you have forgiven someone and force yourself to act as if you have, and no doubt psychically and physically poison yourself at the same time, as the pain continues to fester within you. When you have released all the pain, anger, fear, resentment etc connected to the person who has hurt you, then forgiveness is no longer relevant. If you no longer hold resentment against a person, then what is there to forgive?

Thus I find that doing a Relationship Healing does away with the need for any type of formal forgiveness.

Chapter 10

Toning

Toning is a sound made with the human voice, an "ah" sound. You open your mouth and let a continuous sound come out, breathing through your open mouth when necessary. It is important to take in-breaths quickly so the break in the sound is very short. The sound should be at an even tempo.

Discovering Toning was one of the breakthroughs of my healing career. Let me share with you how I discovered it. I was in my local Kwik Fit trying to get the puncture in one of the tyres of my car mended. I was short of time. I was second in the queue, 30 minutes later, I was still second in the queue. There were various Kwik Fit men around not doing anything constructive. I felt an energy in my body, seeking an exit, I opened my mouth and screamed, the energy rippled up my body and out, but by the end of the scream, I could still feel an unreleased bit in my right hand. So I screamed again and got that bit out. As is typical in England, everyone ignored me. As I was screaming, I noticed a couple of army blokes rolling a huge wheel across the tarmac, they did not falter in any way, they just kept rolling the wheel. The result of my scream was that someone came and mended my puncture and then refused to take any money for it, maybe they wanted me out of the place as quickly as possible. Later a friend said to me: "You mistook the meaning of Kwik Fit, you thought it meant a place where tyres and exhausts were mended quickly, but actually it is a place where one has a fit quickly!"

Later I realized how much better I felt. I had not felt so good for weeks; the screams had done me more good than anything I had done in awhile. The good effects from the screams lasted for two weeks. Around this time, I chanced upon a book called

"Toning" by Laurel Elizabeth Keyes. I bought it and read it. It taught you how to use your voice to make yourself healthy physically. For me it had two downsides. First you were supposed to do it standing up, I decided to give that a miss, and started doing it sitting down. Secondly you had to be musical to do it which is beyond my capabilities, so I decided to use it in a different way, I decided to use it to release stuck emotions. It was one of the best decisions I have ever made. I started to use it to help me give up smoking; I used it to release my emotions, mainly anger, which caused me to smoke in the first place.

Using Toning to Give Up Smoking

Let me tell you exactly how I used Toning to give up smoking, in case you would like to try it yourself. I told myself that whenever I felt like a cigarette, I would wait until I could feel an emotion very strongly, and then I would feel that emotion and Tone until the emotion left me and then I could have a cigarette. I tried to do this every time I felt a desire for a smoke at home. Gradually the time between desires for cigarettes got longer and longer. When it had reached two days I was able to give up smoking fairly painlessly.

The Toning sessions lasted around an hour each. Often as I Toned releasing the emotion I was feeling, I would feel myself go back in time, to an earlier event, from which that emotion had come. Thus my Toning sessions cleared up a lot of past trauma in my life.

*Around this time, my friend, **Veronica**, was having boyfriend trouble. She asked if there was anything I could do to help. I suggested that she came round and we tried Toning for him together. I would like to point out that we Toned to make him whole and healthy, we did not Tone to manipulate his behaviour, as that would have been wrong, and would have attracted negative energy to us. During the session, I had such a dreadful coughing fit that I could* *hardly breathe. Veronica wanted to ring for an ambulance as she thought I was about to die on her, however, I knew the coughing fit was connected in some way to the healing. At the time, I did not have a cough, so the coughing fit was very unexpected.*

The next time Veronica saw her boyfriend, she discovered that the bronchitis that he had had ever since she had first met him had completely gone. Thus my coughing fit had somehow cured his bronchitis. Veronica's relationship with her boyfriend also improved, so the Toning session for him was a success all round.

How to Tone

When you are feeling angry, sad, fearful, guilty or any other negative emotion and that feeling won't go away, go somewhere quiet, open your mouth and make a Toning sound, or an "ah" sound until the feeling goes. If you make the sound for long enough the feeling will go, though it can take up to an hour. It is important that you keep your mouth open throughout, that the sound is continuous, and that you breathe quickly through your open mouth, when required.

Let me give you some examples of the healing power of Toning from the lives of my clients.

__Marina__ came from South America and was a very tricky customer, all normal ideas of good behaviour and honesty were lacking in Marina's life. She was also a very angry lady and this led to her losing her cleaning jobs. I taught her to Tone. She told me that she used to scream with fury at her employer, but now she would grit her teeth, go to the bathroom, lock the door, Tone for half an hour and then return smiling peacefully. Marina managed to keep this job.

One of my clients used to go for drives on the M1 and Tone out his fury, though generally speaking, I would suggest that you do not Tone when driving, as you should be keeping your attention on driving not the Toning!

The real magic in Toning is when it takes you back to an earlier event in this life, or to a past life, then you can heal that original event with the Toning and your emotional problem does not reoccur as a result.

Maggie's problem was that she could not eat in public without being sick. At a restaurant or at a party she would become panicky, and would either have to go home or be sick. This was causing great problems between Maggie and her boyfriend, who was getting very close to dumping her. I asked Maggie to get in touch with the last time she had had to be taken home in the middle of a meal, feel what she felt then and make the Toning sound. As a result of this, Maggie remembered her father making a huge and embarrassing scene in public at her first birthday party as a young adult. I then did a Relationship Healing between Maggie and her father for this event, followed by a replay of the party without her father making a scene during it.

Maggie left me feeling renewed; she now understood why it was she could not handle eating in public. She went home and explained the whole situation to her boyfriend, who was very understanding. Maggie never again felt panicky during a meal.

Julie had been with her boyfriend for two years, and suddenly could not bear him to make love to her. It was only a matter of time before her relationship would end because of this. The thing that was really upsetting Julie was that this happened with all her boyfriends and always at the two year mark. I suggested that the next time he tried to make love to her and she could not handle it, that she Toned instead, found out where the cause came from and then came back to visit me to have it sorted out.

Julie did this, and remembered that when she was about ten, her best friend's father, whom she had known for two years, had fondled her sexually. She went home and told her mother who just made some comment about it being a thing that adults do. I helped Julie to heal the event by doing a Relationship Healing between Julie and her best friend's father. After this healing, Julie felt perfectly comfortable when her boyfriend wanted to make love to her.

Peggy *was feeling emotional and did not know why. These emotional bouts came and went and she found life very difficult during these periods. She came to see me during one of her attacks. Through Toning she remembered being sexually abused by her elder brother when she was a child. She was amazed that she had forgotten it, particularly as it had happened many times over a six-year period. I did a Relationship Healing between Peggy and her elder brother. This enabled Peggy to confront her brother later and as a result a healing took place between them, and their rather bad relationship took a definite turn for the better. Their improved relationship had positive repercussions throughout Peggy's family and her emotional bouts receded.*

Helen *had been seeing me for a while to sort out various problems when one day she turned up for a session saying she was having a bad day with one of her legs. I asked her to tell me about it. She told me that periodically throughout her life, one of her legs would become weak and painful, and it became difficult for her to walk. She had been to various doctors over the years, but none of them could find anything wrong with her leg. When the problem came on, it would stay for a few days and then get better; it happened once or twice every month.*

I asked Helen to lie down, I put my hands on her leg, asked her to feel the pain and to Tone. As a result Helen went back into a past life where she was in leg irons. I helped Helen to heal this past life. At the end of the session Helen's leg was pain free. I continued to see Helen for a few more months and her leg problem did not return.

I used to suffer from anxiety about not breaking the law with my car. I always parked my car in an approved area, making sure it was always the right number of inches away from the pavement, I never parked on yellow lines, I never drove too fast, or after

Know That You Are Loved

drinking alcohol. I was always double checking my parking permit and tax disc to make sure that they were not about to fall off the windscreen. My life with my car was very time consuming. One day I got tired of my fear of authority, so I taught a friend of mine my method of Toning and paid her to heal me of my fears.

Feeling my fear and Toning at the same time I remembered my school days in a convent in Twickenham. I remembered how we were ridiculed if we took more than three minutes to change into gym clothes, or if we had forgotten to put a name tag on one of our socks. I released my fear of the teachers by Toning and telling the teachers what I thought of them. After a few sessions of this I was able to break a few laws, at one point I even caught myself driving the wrong way up a one-way street!

Releasing long-term stuck emotions is very healing. Releasing anger energizes you to such an extent that you can be on a high for up to three weeks afterwards. Releasing sadness can be tiring, but you recover quite quickly. Some people believe that releasing sadness through crying gives you a headache. From personal experience and that of my clients, we have found that a good old boo hoo does not give you a headache, however, crying but trying not to cry at the same time is a sure route to a bad headache. Let go and cry, no headache. Hold on and cry, bad headache. Releasing fear is absolutely exhausting. When I released the fear of my teachers, I could not stand up for about three hours afterwards. I was shattered for days, unable to work. Long term, releasing fear is the most rewarding, as for years afterwards you remember how debilitating life used to be when you had the fear, and how free you feel now that you no longer have it.

During Toning sessions, clients often need to stop and have a good cry, or have a coughing fit, or yawn deeply or hiccup or burp. I always tell the client to let go and do what is wanting to happen. Crying obviously releases sadness, coughing tends to release anger, deep yawning is a sign that an old and stuck emotion is being cleared up. When a client is carrying fear, they are normally very cold at the start of the session, then as the fear is released they often shake, and then return to normal temperature immediately the fear has gone. As for hiccupping or burping I am not sure exactly which emotion they are releasing. Occasionally clients release their stuck emotions through a laughing fit, which is great. Sometimes clients cry for a long time, or laugh, not knowing why they are crying or laughing. A healing always occurs when this happens; we just do not know what it is from the client's past that has been healed.

Chapter 11

Finding the Emotional Cause of Physical Problems

Another method of healing I learnt in my early days as a healer was to look for the emotional cause behind the physical problem and heal that. I found that most physical problems had an emotional problem behind them. Usually the emotional problem could be found in the present life of the client; only occasionally did the cause come from a past life. I would describe it to clients like this, "Your emotional problem is like water, when it gets bad enough it turns to ice and then you have a physical problem. The healing lies in turning that ice back into water and then letting it flow out of you." I would help the client find the emotional problem behind his physical problem, and then help him to release it.

The cause of an ailment seems to be roughly the same from person to person. To learn more about the causes of various physical problems, see Louise L. Hay's book, "Heal Your Body".

Working with a number of women who had fibroids, I found that most of them had had abortions which they had later regretted, and most of them were trying and failing to get pregnant. One woman had had a miscarriage and although she had had children since, she felt she wanted the child who had been miscarried. She wanted to get back the child she had lost. Thus most of the women were growing fibroids in their wombs instead of the child they desperately wanted. Those who had had abortions felt that not being able to have a baby was a punishment from God for their earlier abortions.

In the Relationship Healings I did with the women and their aborted or miscarried babies, in every case the aborted or miscarried baby said he was fine and was only supposed to have had a short life as a foetus. Having healed the mother's relationship with her lost baby and having helped her to release the emotions concerning wanting a baby and failing to get pregnant, the fibroids tended to go.

Meera came to see me for an emergency healing. She had fibroids and had been bleeding for a month. As a result she was exhausted and rather anaemic. The day before she had collapsed in the street and been taken to hospital. The doctors told her that if she collapsed in the street again they would take out her womb. During the healing I asked Meera to look for a tap marked "blood" and then to turn it off. Meera did this. She came back a few days later for another healing, and told me she had stopped bleeding one hour after she had left me.

Six months later Meera returned to see me as her fibroids were causing trouble again. This time I helped her do Relationship Healings with the babies that she had aborted, and to look into what was going on emotionally in her present relationship. A few weeks later Meera went into hospital for a pre-arranged operation to have 13 fibroids removed. When she came round after her operation, she was met by a rather embarrassed surgeon, who told her that he could not find a fibroid anywhere. All 13 fibroids had disappeared.

George told me that the ganglion on his wrist had grown and he was going to go to the hospital to have it removed for the third time. I suggested he try a healing. I sat holding George's wrist and concentrated on sending white light to the ganglion so as to break it up. Three days later George rang me to say his ganglion had vanished. He was feeling rather freaked out about it, I told him not to call it back!

A few months later, George's ganglion returned, I removed it again.

After a few more months George's ganglion returned again. I realized at this point that we would have to heal the cause if George's *ganglion was to go forever. I asked George what in his life was slightly inconvenient but did not cause him a lot of anguish; the ganglion fitted this description, but what else did? George said that the only thing he could think of was his ex-wife living in his house. I told him that he really should get her to move out but he explained that he could not afford to keep his ex-wife in the manner to which she was accustomed, unless she lived in his house. As he was determined to hang on to his ex-wife, I told him he would have to keep his ganglion. A few months after this, George's ex-wife left of her own accord, followed by George's ganglion, which to the best of my knowledge has never returned.*

Clare suffered from asthma, but only while living in the UK. Her husband would spend years at a time working in a third world country. Abroad Clare never suffered from asthma, but once back in this country the asthma returned. I asked Clare what possible advantage the asthma gave her. After quite a bit of thought, she told me that it gave her time off work. While with her husband in the third world countries Clare could not work as she couldn't get a working visa. She also had servants: a cook, a nanny, a chauffeur and a cleaner. As we looked at Clare's situation, Clare realized that she didn't enjoy work, but felt morally obliged to go to work when the opportunity presented itself. She would not contemplate my suggestion that she gave up work entirely. She would rather continue to tolerate asthma while in the UK. Of course the ideal answer would have been for Clare to have found some work that she really enjoyed, but she was determined to continue with her present job.

Frederick had diabetes; he had had it since he was a small boy. When he first came to see me, he was injecting himself with an average of 90 units of insulin per day. He saw me over a six-month period, by which time his insulin requirements had been reduced to between 20 and 30 units per day. At this point Frederick's job moved him to another part of England and Frederick stopped visiting me.

Curiously I have never yet met a person with diabetes who did not have a difficult relationship with his mother. In Frederick's case his mother was very controlling and his father allowed his wife to control everything and everybody. In my sessions with Frederick I taught him how to stand up to his mother.

*When **Josephine** first came to see me she looked terrible. She explained that she had had about 12 early miscarriages, and the one child she had managed to carry for full term had died a few hours after birth. As a result of this she and her husband had decided to adopt, but she was finding the process very off-putting. I suggested to Josephine that she put the adoption process on hold while she tried some healing with me. Josephine came to see me once a week for five months, by which time she was three months pregnant with a healthy child. She has since gone on to have three more children, and now can't imagine what it was like to long for a child!*

Josephine's mother had tried to abort Josephine in the early months of her pregnancy using various old wives methods. The desire of Josephine's mother to abort her baby had got lodged in Josephine and this had brought about all of Josephine's early miscarriages. The baby that Josephine had carried full term had tried to miscarry on several occasions, but the doctors had managed to save it and she had spent most of the last six months of her pregnancy in hospital.

I helped Josephine do a Relationship Healing with her mother and confront the many times that her mother had tried to abort her and the times she had been extremely unkind to Josephine as she was growing up. I also did Relationship Healings between Josephine and her miscarried babies and her dead child.

*Many years ago while I was staying at Shantivanam Ashram in South India, a young woman called **Sheila**, who was also staying there, got such bad backache that she was reduced to crawling around on all fours. One day she crawled in to see me. I laid her on my bed, put my hands on the most painful parts of her back, and asked her to feel the pain and see where it took her. Sheila remem-*

bered the death of her dog, when she was ten, and how her family did not allow her to mourn it. I did a Relationship Healing between Sheila and her dog, and between Sheila and her parents regarding the death of the dog. Sheila walked out of my room pain free and the pain did not return.

You might ask what triggered the cause of Sheila's backache, why did the death of her dog lie dormant for so many years and then suddenly turn up in agonizing backache. Shantivanam is a place of healing, where people's hidden problems are brought to the surface. Also just before Sheila's backache came on, she had found a dead squirrel. So I assume that the sight of the dead squirrel activated Sheila's hidden pain from the death of her dog.

For many people, backache is a wonderful excuse not to have to work. A few people, in this situation have been to see me, but after a couple of sessions have reduced their pain, they decide not to return. The excuse being that they cannot afford to see me as they are not working. I would point out that if they got rid of their back pain they would be able to get back to work but I often got the feeling that they did not want to get back to work!

Many years ago, I decided to move and I put my flat on the market. The day I accepted an offer my back seized up. I was in total agony. I lay down on the floor, felt the pain in my back and let it take me to its cause. I realized that I was terrified of losing my flat. I did not want to sell it. Having discovered this, my backache improved tremendously but did not go completely. A few days later, my buyer pulled out, I felt an overwhelming sense of relief, and my backache went completely. I withdrew my flat from the market, and have never tried to sell it since.

Many years ago, a mother brought her seven-year old child to see me, who had 30 verrucas on her foot. Over the previous three years various Harley Street doctors had attempted to remove the verrucas but they always came back. (The methods of removal had also been very painful.) By observing the child I noticed that she was always swinging the leg with the verrucas on it, as if she wanted to kick someone. I sat her on my healing chair, asked her to relax, and then asked her whom she wanted to kick? She told me the names of three school friends. I asked the child to imagine her school friends in her mind and to kick them. I also introduced the child to her guardian angel for protection and friendship. I saw the child three times and by the beginning of the third session 20 of the verrucas had gone. At the start of this session, the child complained of feeling cold, so I wrapped her in two blankets while her mother sunbathed in a bikini on my balcony. During this session, having beaten up various school friends in her mind, she then told me she could see Mary, I assumed that Mary was another school friend, but then she said, "And Jesus." So I told her to ask Jesus to touch her foot and to heal the verrucas. "Done that," she said a couple of minutes later and then she threw off the blankets and stated that her session was finished. A few days later the rest of the verrucas went, I spoke to the child six years later and she told me that the verrucas had never returned.

I would like to point out that encouraging a client, in their mind, to kick, punch or otherwise beat up someone they are angry with does not harm the person concerned in any way. The intention is what matters. If the intention of the session is healing, then the method used will not harm another. Occasionally clients who are angry with someone tell me that they do not want to beat the person up in their mind, as they do not want to injure that person. I point out that they are already injuring that person with their anger. By releasing that anger, they will be doing the person concerned a favour, because as they release their anger towards that person, the damage that they were doing will cease. When you carry unresolved anger towards someone, that anger can and will cause problems for the person you are angry with so releasing that anger is very important. Being a very sensitive person myself, I can feel when someone is angry with me, I usually know who the person is, as I can sense their presence attached to their anger. I try to avoid making people angry with me, as I know it will cause me problems that I would rather do without.

To see how to rescue yourself from the anger of another, see Chapter 14.

Chapter 12

Healing Cars and Houses

When I have problems with my house or my car, finding the emotional cause in my personal life and healing that, enables my house or car problem to get rectified for free or for only a token payment. The same principle could no doubt be applied to other things in one's life, but I have only had experience with my house and my car.

When something you own goes wrong or won't work, look to see what it represents in your life. See if you can find an emotional problem which reflects it and then do a healing. Then it's a matter of waiting a few hours or days, to see how the object you own is going to get itself better, without needing to pay a large sum of money to get it mended. The best way of explaining this is to give some examples.

When I was 19 my mother bought me an old Post Office van; I wanted a moped, but my mother thought I would be safer in a car. Right from the beginning the van had starting problems. Almost every morning it would stop on hills and dangerous bends and then refuse to restart. Over the next few years I had numerous parts replaced by various mechanics. Finally a garage in Reading discovered that the wire that connected the car to its engine was faulty, it cost 50p to replace and from then on the van usually started.

In the mid-eighties I bought a second-hand car and was promised that it did not have starting problems. Within five days of buying it, it refused to start and had to go back to the garage from which I had bought it. Over the next few months, I had more starting problems with it.

By now I was on the healing path and decided to look at my

own life. I realized I had starting problems, particularly in the mornings; I could never get going. A lot of this was to do with being unhappy and not wanting to get started in the mornings. I used Toning and Relationship Healings to sort out many of the causes of my unhappiness and tried to look forward to each day, and to get going in the mornings. As I improved my car got better too. None of the second-hand cars that I subsequently bought had starting problems.

Many years ago the gears on one of my cars went. I drove it in second gear at about 15 miles an hour to a garage near my home. At the time the car was full of my friends, who started to window shop as I drove along slowly. All the other traffic around started hooting and yelling at me, thinking that I was driving slowly so my friends could window shop! The garage told me that new gears plus fitting would cost £100. At that time £100 was a lot of money for me. I sat at home wondering what to do about the situation, while the car sat forlornly in the garage.

I decided to look at what gears represented in my life. I decided it was something to do with changing direction, and being able to change the speed at which I acted to suit the situation in hand. I realized I was very bad at this. Due to my years in India, I did everything slowly whether it suited the situation in hand or not; I was permanently stuck in the equivalent of second gear in my life. I did some healing on myself, exactly what I cannot remember now, but shortly after I had finished, a man from the garage rang me up and told me he had just been to the car tip for someone else, and had picked me up an almost brand new set of gears. He told me he would fit them for £20, and not charge me for the actual gears as he had picked them up for free. I thanked him profusely and asked him to go ahead and fix them.

Some years later the clutch on my car became noisy and changing gear became difficult. I was about to go on holiday and decided to deal with the problem on my return. While I was away

I considered what a faulty clutch might mean in my life. Rather like faulty gears, I felt it had to do with the ability to alter the pace of my life. By that time I had mastered the art of doing things quickly when required, but was not very good at slowing down or taking time for myself. This holiday fulfilled that need and I returned home to a silent clutch in perfect working order.

Towards the beginning of my healing path, before I had learnt about releasing one's emotions through Toning, I was suffering from a lot of anger, and only knew how to release it by yelling my head off, which was not very easy at the time as I was living in someone else's house. One day my car radiator blew up. I had it mended. Next day the mended radiator blew up. I had a reconstituted radiator put in. Next day it blew up. I had a new radiator put in, next day that blew up. By this time both the garage and I had had enough. I went somewhere quiet and yelled all my anger out, the garage put in another new radiator but did not charge me for it. From then on my radiators behaved, and I always released my anger at the first sign of trouble.

In life water represents emotions, still waters mean one's emotions are at peace, storms and other types of agitated water represent emotions which need to be released. Fire represents anger. My radiators blew up because they got too hot, that is the water in the radiator got too hot and blew up the radiator. Water getting too hot represented my anger, which needed to be released in a safe way.

One of my cousins was floating through life a few years ago. She was not in charge, not at the steering wheel you might say. She had her steering wheel stolen and within three months the new steering wheel was also stolen. Both times she was rescued by the AA who had difficulty believing that this could happen to the same person twice within a three month period.

Let me tell you about three miraculous healings regarding cars. Rebecca dropped her children off at school one day. Then her car would not start. Various children's fathers tried to start it, as did the school caretaker, but to no avail. Rebecca rang the AA, and sat in her car to await their arrival. At 11 a.m. a Catholic nun with healing abilities, arrived at the school. She saw Rebecca sitting in her car, and asked what she was doing there. Rebecca explained the situation. The nun put her hand on the windscreen, looked up to heaven, and said, "Dear God, your daughter wants to get home, please start her car." The nun then asked Rebecca to try to start the car. Rebecca refused on the grounds that it was pointless. The nun said to Rebecca, "Either you try it dear, or I will." Rebecca tried the engine and it purred into life.

Rebecca told me that she drove the car home, had lunch, went shopping, took the shopping home, collected the children from school, took them home, then took the car to the garage, at which point it stopped completely and would not start again. The man at the garage told Rebecca that there was something seriously wrong with her car, and that there was no explanation as to how she had been driving it around all day.

The second miracle happened to one of my second-hand cars. It was leaking oil, at the rate of needing a pint a week. I took it to a garage near my mother in Somerset. As it was a Sunday none of the mechanics were there, however, the 18-year-old son of the owners put it on the car lift, rose the car in the air, looked at it from below and told me that mending the leak would cause more problems, expensive ones, and he suggested my cheapest option was to continue to buy a pint of oil a week. From that day forward my car stopped leaking oil; it could go for six months before it needed a top up. A year or so later, I visited the same garage, and told the boy's mother about the miraculous effect on my car, as a result of her son just looking at it. She told me that other people had reported other such miracles, she seemed almost sad about it; I suppose that if you earn your living from mending people's cars, and your son heals them in minutes by just looking at them, it could be very annoying.

The third miracle concerns another car that would not start. I had taken a team of healers to Belgium to release spirits and negative energy from a castle near Brussels. Some friends of the owners of the castle needed to get back to Paris but their car wouldn't start. It gave out that noise that means the battery is completely flat and either needs a new battery or a jumpstart. Gareth, one of the members of my team, put his hand on the windscreen, looked up to heaven and chanted to the Goddess Themis in ancient Greek. When he had finished, the car purred into life as if there was nothing wrong with it, and the lady and her daughter got back to Paris without any more trouble.

I remember years ago, when a male friend of mine was having difficulty getting his car to start, I suggested he kissed the windscreen, he looked at me as if I was mad. Having tried yelling, kicking, swearing and pleading, he finally tried kissing the windscreen and the car agreed to start! I believe that as we humans are made of energy, when we get emotional our energy becomes stronger and is able to interfere with the electrical workings of things that we own. I have personally found that when feeling angry, it is not the right moment to turn a light on or off, unless I want to go light bulb shopping!

Now let me tell you about how your out of control emotions can negatively effect your home. My main experience in the home has been water problems. I have found when one is carrying unresolved emotional problems one tends to have water difficulties that lead to numerous plumbing bills. The first flat I owned had water problems for the entire time I lived there, except for the two years that I was in India, during which time my lodgers had not one water problem. Most of my problems were in some way connected to the water tank in the roof. Every time I had a ballcock replaced I was told it should last for at least 20, if not for 50 years. Each time I was lucky if it lasted six months!

Now in those days I had emotional problems in all directions but never released them. In my flat I had to keep a cap on my feelings most of the time because I had a lodger and because the walls between me and the neighbours were not exactly soundproof, whereas in India I was releasing my emotions the whole time. I tended to lose my temper at least twice a day and if I got upset I would burst into tears. So in India I released my emotions freely but as soon as I returned home with my emotional problems pent up, the roof started to leak. During the five years that I lived in that flat, the water tank overflowed countless times, causing two bedroom ceilings to fall in and five ballcock replacements. I also had to have a new roof.

By the time I had moved into my present flat, I had started on my healing path and had found suitable outlets for my emotions, this resulted in me being free of ongoing water problems.

The problem with healing your car or house via healing yourself is that sometimes you cannot work out what the problem with the car or house reflects in your life. A friend of mine suggests that the central heating system reflects your heart where relationships are concerned. Electrical objects blowing up are often the result of suppressed anger. Water leaking represents unresolved sorrow. Water causing a lot of damage represents suppressed anger where relationships are concerned.

Sometimes I find that the plumbing or garage bill would be less than the healing bill so I take that path. However, unless I am healed, the problem usually returns at a later date.

I would be very interested to hear from anyone who has had their house, car or other object miraculously healed by finding and healing a problem in their own life. Please contact me through my websites; www.knowthatyouareloved.com and www.philena.co.uk.

Chapter 13

The Story Method

The Story Method is another method of healing, which I discovered by chance. Some years ago I woke up one morning with agonizing pains in the soles of both my feet. It took an age to get out of bed, as standing caused pain beyond anything I had ever experienced. It took me half an hour to pluck up the courage to take the one step needed to turn off my alarm clock.

After three or four days of crawling around my flat, I had had enough. The pain reminded me of the pain experienced by The Little Mermaid when she was given legs and allowed to marry her prince. I found a version of The Little Mermaid. I discovered that in The Little Mermaid's story it was her legs that hurt, not her feet, but I decided to go ahead, change the ending of her story and see what happened. I went into deep relaxation, pretended I was The Little Mermaid and changed the ending of the story; so that she was happy with her prince, and her legs and feet were pain free. After I had finished I tried to stand up and my feet were pain free. The pain never returned.

Some years later I discovered a different method of using a story for healing. I would look for, say, a loving, caring, mother in a book, film or fairy story. I had great success from films that I happened to watch on television. I would take the loving mother out of the film, and substitute her for my real mother in my mind, then replay my life differently to the way it had actually happened. When you change your past in your head, your present changes, followed by a changed future. They say that your mind cannot tell the difference between what actually happened and what it thinks happened, therefore changing what your mind thinks happened can bring about changes in how you relate to life, and therefore your present and your future changes.

Over the years I have told myself many different stories; often various versions of one story would go on for years. I was always one of the main characters in the stories. Let me tell you how I made changes in my life by consciously changing one of my stories.

In the late eighties I was trying to buy myself a flat in London. I had found the ideal place and then just before exchange of contracts, another person offered my seller £2000 more and all the paperwork ground to a halt. I was distracted with worry; all I could do was pray. It came to me that I should get the different characters in my main story to forgive each other. It seemed so bizarre that I ignored the idea. Three days later when I was even more distracted, it came more strongly, "get the characters in my story to forgive each other".

At this time I was teaching mathematics part-time and when I had about 45 minutes of free time I found an empty room where I was unlikely to be disturbed. I sat down on the floor with an iced bun, a cup of tea and a cigarette with the intention of getting about eight different characters in my story to forgive each other. I had no time for my characters to argue about it, they had to just get on and do it. Releasing their various emotions would have to be done at a later date. When all eight characters had forgiven each other, I stood up and promptly fell over! To my amazement I had been in such a deep trance that I was quite dizzy. I went to teach my class and the children told me they thought I was on drugs!

When I got home, my lawyer rang me to say that he had spoken to the seller's lawyer and the seller had decided to go ahead and contracts would be exchanged first thing Monday morning. My mother also rang to offer me the extra £2000. On the Monday morning the contracts were exchanged without needing to use the extra £2000 that my mother had offered.

As a result of getting all the characters of my main story to forgive each other, I never managed to really enjoy telling myself that story again, as it had lost its punch. Over the next few years I played around with other stories and changed them so that they were happy stories rather than unhappy stories, with resulting interesting changes in my real life. A bit like Symbolic Visualization, where one changes a not-okay symbol into a good one, I found that by changing my rather sad stories into happy ones my life changed for the better. With Symbolic Visualization, you know what you are trying to change; when I changed my stories, I had no idea what would change until it happened. But I used to find that the change in my real life would occur approximately three days after I had done the healing.

Chapter 14

Releasing Yourself from Curses and Psychic Attack

One method of releasing yourself from the anger of another is to discuss it with them. Do not do this if you have just had a row with the person concerned. If you believe that someone is angry with you and you do not know why, ringing them up and asking them what is going on can be educational as well as very healing. But do not call if feeling angry yourself, do not start to blame the other person and do keep very calm, otherwise you may make the situation worse.

Another method of releasing yourself from the anger of another, when you know who that person is, is a Relationship Healing. In this healing you are likely to find out why the person is angry with you and what you can do about it.

While I was working on this book I was verbally and psychically attacked by a friend and colleague. Within a five-day period I went from total emotional shock, through bodily shock with physical pain, to feeling perfectly all right and emotionally healthy. I rescued myself by firstly remembering that I was loved and by knowing that because I was loved the psychic attack would not be able to harm me. I also cut all energetic ties with the person concerned. Below I explain how to successfully cut these ties.

Cutting the Ties

Using any tune, sing something like:

Choppety chop, choppety chop,

Chop, chop, chop,

I'm cutting the ties with (the name of the relevant person).

Sing it over and over again, while imagining cutting cords that are connecting the two of you. Singing raises the vibration and makes the cutting of the cords far easier and quicker than doing it by visualization during a healing session. The side effect of singing is that it makes you feel good, both while you are doing it and afterwards. When you feel that you have successfully cut the cords, ask the angels to remove the cords from you, clean out the parts of you where the cords were connected and then to fill any spaces with golden light. You may also do this for the other person if you wish. Then ask the angels to transform the cords into something beautiful for the good of the planet; it is not good to leave psychic debris lying around. Thank the angels for their help. Next call back to yourself any energy that is yours that the other person is holding. Imagine beams of light or energy rushing towards you from the other person, with your name written on them. Then send back to the other person any of his or her energy that you are holding, again imagine beams of light leaving you and rushing back to the other person with his or her name on them.

Another method of rescuing yourself from psychic attack was taught to one of my clients by a Native American shaman; it is now known amongst my clients as the Tea Towel method. The victim of psychic attack would give the attacker a bolt of cotton cloth wrapped up in a ribbon. Nowadays a bolt of cotton cloth would be very expensive and the receiver probably would not know what to do with it. The idea is to give the attacker a piece of 100 per cent cotton wrapped up in a ribbon of any colour and of any material. In the UK the cheapest 100 per cent cotton you can buy is a tea towel, which is how the Tea Towel method got its name.

So if you know who is attacking you, give that person a tea towel, or something else made of 100 per cent cotton wrapped up in a ribbon. Do not wrap the towel and ribbon in paper, just give it as it is. If the person lives too far away for you to visit them, then you may put your piece of cotton and ribbon in an envelope and send it by post. Many of my clients have told me that if the receiver were to know who had sent them the tea towel, they would send it straight back. In cases like this, I suggest you write the name and address of the person with your left hand if you are right-handed, and with your right hand if you are left-handed. (The writing of your other hand tends to be totally unrecognisable.)

Over the years many of my clients have rung me to tell me how successful the Tea Towel method was for them. Some had to wait a few weeks for results while their tea towel slowly crossed the world by ship en route to some African or Latin American country. I have never had anyone tell me that it did not work.

People from all sorts of backgrounds have tried this method with great success. Many people have found it very embarrassing to put into action. I remember one retired businessman telling me how he gave one to his mother. He said, "I just held it out, while looking the other way. It's been a great success, she has been treating me very well ever since."

The client who was taught this method by the Native American shaman did not know who was sending her bad energy, so she and her husband spent a month driving 50 tea towels wrapped in ribbons around England, giving one to every person they knew. They told me it was a great success and really worth the effort and the cost of the tea towels and the petrol.

The next question is likely to be: how or why does it work? Is it magic? What is magic? I believe magic to be a science as yet undiscovered by scientists. I believe it works for two reasons. Firstly cotton is 100 per cent absorbent, so on the etheric level it absorbs the bad energy which is being sent, even if the attacker does not know consciously who it was who sent them the tea towel. Also it is difficult to continue to send someone bad energy after they have given you a present. As tea towels tend to be very useful, the receiver is likely to be constantly reminded that it was you who gave them that tea towel as an unexpected gift, it not being their birthday or Christmas.

There are two other methods which I have learnt from other psychics, which are cheaper and take less effort. However, they can potentially have negative side effects. The first method requires you to know who it is who is sending you the bad energy. For this method write the name of the person concerned on a tiny bit of paper, and put it in one of the holes of an ice tray, fill it with water and put in the freezer. The idea is that this freezes the bad energy the person is sending you, but does not harm the person in any way. The obvious disadvantage to this, is that during your next party, when you tell a friend to get the ice out of the freezer, it will not be long before someone will be asking you why so and so's name is floating around in their gin and tonic. The less obvious disadvantage of this method is that if there is an unexpected power cut, or you just decide one day to throw that ice cube out, then the negative energy that was being held away from you suddenly descends on you when you least expect it.

The other method is to put a photograph of yourself on a plate on a table, and to put a crucifix, piece of sage or jade on top of it; crucifixes, sage and jade protect you from negative energy. I can personally vouch that this method works, but you cannot leave it on your table forever. The time will come when you need to remove it; this is the point when things can get dangerous. If you just remove the plate, the bad energy that has been held off can suddenly descend upon you. The way I deal with the situation is to do a meditation, and ask God for white light protection as I throw away the sage, and clear up the plate, and for that white light protection to continue to be with me in the coming days.

Here is an example of when sudden removal of protection caused problems. My mother used to keep fresh flowers in front of a statue of Our Lady to protect her children from car accidents. When my mother moved house, for 24 hours there were no flowers in front of Our Lady. During those 24 hours I had a car accident. After my mother's death, I kept fresh flowers in front of Our Lady to protect me from car accidents. One day when I was going away for a couple of weeks, I looked at the flowers in front of Our Lady and realized they were almost dead. I also realized that if I replaced them with fresh flowers, they would also be dead by the time I returned, so I decided not to replace them. A couple of weeks later, I had a car accident. Now in case you think these examples were just coincidences, I would like to point out that over the ten or more years that my mother or I had put flowers in front of Our Lady neither my four sisters nor I had car accidents except for the two mentioned above.

After this second car accident of mine, I decided that putting fresh flowers in front of Our Lady was a bit risky, in case I forgot. So as a back up to the flowers, I put a piece of amethyst in my car, which I cleaned monthly, by washing under the tap and by tapping with a spoon. Tapping a crystal gently with a spoon is a most successful way of cleaning it. There is a known science behind tapping. When you tap a crystal with a spoon or another crystal, the atoms in the crystal jump up and down and any negative energy the crystal is holding gets dislodged. After this I had many years of accident free motoring. Finally this car was written off by a hit and run driver while it was parked and I was sitting at home watching television. I decided not to replace the car and bought a computer instead.

Two other ways of getting yourself released from a curse, psychic attack or the anger of another are to pray for the person concerned, even if you do not know who he or she is, or go to a Spirit Release Practitioner. Let me give you an example of someone I released from a curse.

Adriana came from Latin America, she had been well off and life had been good until the day she sat next to the wrong person on an aeroplane. A complete stranger cursed Adriana, for what reason we do not know, and from that day forward Adriana's life went down hill drastically. When Adriana arrived to see me she was in terrible straits: her landlady wanted to put her rent up, she only earned money through commission and she had had no commissions for over a year; her UK visa had only three weeks left on it and she needed an employer to renew it on her behalf; and her boss's new mistress loathed her and was making trouble between him and Adriana.

I worked with Adriana to remove the curse. In one three-hour session I removed from Adriana's energy field numerous lost elemental spirits who had been sent by the lady on the aeroplane to mess up Adriana's life.

While Adriana was with me having her curse removed, a lady who owed her £10,000 rang her up and left a message to the effect that she was feeling guilty about the money she owed Adriana and would pay a first instalment of £1000 as soon as possible. This debt was ten-years-old.

A few days after my session with Adriana, her landlady changed her mind about putting the rent up. Adriana's boss gave her a salaried job, sorted out her UK visa and because he thought Adriana was looking stressed, sent her to a health farm in Switzerland, for a week, at his expense. The negative influence of Adriana's boss's mistress ceased. In less than two weeks Adriana's life took an amazing turn for the better on all fronts.

When a person's life is not working because they have been genuinely cursed, removing the curse tends to produce rapid results.

Many people who think they have been cursed have not, and other people who do not believe in curses have. It's a funny old world. Many of those who think they have been cursed are looking for a reason outside of themselves to blame for their life not working. These people are needing to work on themselves with the help of a healer or psychotherapist.

Sometimes the cause of a curse lies in a past life. In this case healing the past life can release the curse. Some cases involving past lives can be complicated and the client is likely to need more than one session to be released.

Postscript: I Know That I Am Loved

I would like to end this book with a miraculous experience I had while writing it. I was in India at the time and decided to change the date of my homecoming, so I could spend time in the ashram of a Holy Man, who was well versed in the art of unconditional love. This meant I had to cancel my flight home with a travel agent in the UK and buy a new flight in India. I paid for my new flight with my credit card on the telephone. On the flight I was upgraded to business class, at no cost to myself. Having returned home I could not find the cost of the flight on the credit card that I thought I had used. I could not find it on any of my other credit or debit cards that I might have used. To this day I have not been charged for that flight. I received the rebate for the flight I had cancelled a few months after I had returned home. I was supposed to receive the cost of the flight minus $50; I received the cost of the flight plus $50.

Yes, I know that I am loved. And yes, I remembered to thank the Goddess.

Remember you are loved.
Remember you are loved.
Remember you are loved.

This statement alone, when accepted by your unconscious mind as well as your conscious mind, can change your life for the better, forever.

Remember you are loved; break out of your chrysalis and become the wonderful butterfly you truly are.

Philena Bruce
www.philena.co.uk
www.knowthatyouareloved.com

BOOKS

O is a symbol of the world, of oneness and unity. In different cultures it also means the "eye," symbolizing knowledge and insight. We aim to publish books that are accessible, constructive and that challenge accepted opinion, both that of academia and the "moral majority."

Our books are available in all good English language bookstores worldwide. If you don't see the book on the shelves ask the bookstore to order it for you, quoting the ISBN number and title. Alternatively you can order online (all major online retail sites carry our titles) or contact the distributor in the relevant country, listed on the copyright page.

See our website www.o-books.net for a full list of over 500 titles, growing by 100 a year.

And tune in to myspiritradio.com for our book review radio show, hosted by June-Elleni Laine, where you can listen to the authors discussing their books.